WORLDWATCHER: JACK McLARTY

WORLDWATCHER: JACK McLARTY

FIFTY YEARS 1943-1993

PUBLISHED BY McLARTY'S CHOICE
Portland, Oregon

Copyright © 1995
All Rights Reserved

Editor: Barbara Lever McLarty
Editorial Assistant: Grace McDonald
Designer: Chas. S. Politz/Parabola, Ltd.

Edition of 1500 copies

Library of Congress Card Catalog No. 95-076139

Paperbound ISBN No. 0-9644916-1-3
Clothbound ISBN No. 0-9644916-0-5

Fly leaf: Studio shot of the Artist 1975

Title page: The Artist with a painting from "The Auto Show," Image Gallery 1972

INTRODUCTION

It was in 1953 when I came to Portland as Curator of the Museum, that I met Jack McLarty who was then a teacher in the Museum Art School. The staff of the Museum and the faculty of the School were all members of the Portland Art Association and were very close to each other. It was part of the Museum plan to mount good exhibitions of art which it felt would help the teachers and students in the School and please the people of the Portland community.

One most important show was 101 large paintings from the collection of Walter P. Chrysler, Jr. that was organized by the Portland Art Museum in 1956. The exhibition traveled to eight other museums in the country, ending its tour in 1957 in Boston. The Portland Art Museum printed 15,000 copies of the catalog for the Show which sold so well that we printed a second edition of 11,000. This publication set a very high standard for later Museum publications.

Mr. Thomas Colt, then Director of the Portland Art Museum and a friend of Walter Chrysler, made it possible for us to have this exhibition. Soon afterward, Mr. Colt left the Museum and a new Director, Max Sullivan, was named as his successor. His tenure was brief, and I was named Director in 1960.

During my seven years as Curator I had become very familiar with the work of Jack McLarty. And in 1963 it was decided to hold a Retrospective Exhibition of his work. In the introduction for the catalog for his show, which covered 20 years of work, I wrote, "In presenting this retrospective exhibition of paintings and drawings by Jack McLarty, the Museum gives formal recognition of the quality of his work and his stature and influence in the region."

The major text for the catalog was written by Rachael Griffin, who took my place as Curator of the Museum. She was a long-time friend of McLarty and she had close ties with the Museum Art School. I recommend that interested people read this catalog which is available in the Rex Arragon Library located in the Old Masonic Temple now called the Museum North.

This new book you are now reading comes 30 years after the Retrospective, which means that we are now seeing or reading about a half century of Jack McLarty's work. You will see and enjoy his provocative insights and witty concerns with man that are handled with most meaningful skill.

Francis J. Newton
former Director, Portland Art Museum

Portrait of the Artist by Joseph Solman, New York 1942
Collection Paul Solman, Boston

THE METAPHORICAL ART OF JACK McLARTY

Rachael Griffin, Curator, Portland Art Museum
Northwest Review, *University of Oregon   Fall-Winter 1960*

Jack McLarty's paintings have won no easy popularity. Many react negatively to the relentless neon color of the earlier works and are not won over by the paler tints and half-obscured, proliferating imagery of the later paintings. But, chiefly there is a quite natural resistance to the disquieting suggestion, found in most of McLarty's paintings, that our lives are – underneath – chaotic, empty, and desperate. The "delight" content in McLarty paintings is low, compared with that of the nature-poets of Northwest painting or the non-objective art intended chiefly as a "music for the optic nerve."

The fact remains that they are often the most compelling works in a group exhibition and that they are clearly the work of an original and uncompromising mind. That portion of the art-loving public which sees the role of the artist as more complex than the administering of enlightened pleasure finds the statements of McLarty valid – especially so in a period when so much art addresses itself only to those states of mind or feeling which respond to configurations having no clear analogues in the visual world. Paintings which tell us "something we have not known before" about our lives or the psychological climate of our times must draw upon such potent images as the figure, the mask, a room, animals, a ship, a river, bridges, with which human thoughts and feelings have for so long been entangled. *The more original the handling of this imagery, the more interesting the statement* (emphasis added). In McLarty's painting, the import, borne to us through a great variety of images in unsettling combinations, is often painful and shocking. Yet there is no question of the paintings being "tracts" or of the imagery standing in the way of pure expressive form....When the import shifts in emphasis over the years, McLarty's imagery changes and with it appears a corresponding change in color, shapes, and total appearance of the canvas.

The first one-man exhibition of McLarty paintings was held in 1945. The theme of most of these (early) paintings is the city, often the city at night; the compositions, in general, turn on strong parallel vertical axes, the tonal contrasts are strong, with many structural elements in black. Buildings are compressed in order to be contained whole within the picture, and so opened that we see the garish goings-on inside...the metaphorical images are easily read. But many of these images will appear later with new overtones and clusters of meanings ...The man on crutches, the Watcher, the Outsider, may be

seen as the protagonist – the Outsider, in another guise, appears later in McLarty's work. The stout figure of the news vendor is protected by the Umbrella – still a favorite metaphor of the Artist...figures in the street...exist in private worlds; in the night club the merrymakers persuade themselves, for a moment, that they are not alone. Throughout the painting faces are obliterated, averted, or shadowed. There is something of the air of tableau about this and other early McLartys, of action stilled, emotions set. The space of the paintings is hollow and unified like a stage set. Few paintings after the 1940s will present so ambiguous a space or an iconography so clearly legible....

Jack McLarty says he was a silent onlooker as a child, not taking part in the games of other children. Perhaps this years-long role sharpened the powers of observation and the imaginative insights which we see in his work – his separateness encouraging him to look beneath the surface. In any case, he is an astute and sensitive observer and it seems natural to him that ideas which develop out of topical events and scenes should appear in his work. The themes of the 1950s – the Rose Festival, carnivals, playgrounds, sports and others – intertwine and overlap in the paintings as the decade advances and the work gains in depth and complexity....

The works about children are difficult to discuss briefly; but they are important and should not be neglected. We are slow to discern the suggestions they make because they touch a fenced-off part of our consciousness where only platitudinous images are acceptable. Many of McLarty's child figures are not easily acceptable, but there is nothing so simple here as the proposal that children are capable of monstrous acts and imaginings; or that childhood is a cruel and tragic time, much of which we have made haste to forget. It is rather the suggestion that the world of children is *separate* (emphasis added), that all we know about it is what they choose to tell or inadvertently reveal, and that these glancing lights are often so puzzling and unsettling that we forget them or make suitable substitutions...the toys, play equipment, costumes, and preoccupations of children will be found often in later paintings. The little boy in *King of the River* stands in the formal swirls of his torrent, holding aloft a crazy, broken umbrella, two ribs of which strike up against a yellow moon. The color scheme, limited to yellows and heavy greys, is not

Opposite: Rachael Griffin and Donald Jenkins at the Portland Art Museum preparing the work of Jack McLarty for his Retrospective, September 1963

playful, and there is an atmosphere of something fearful impending which seems at first to threaten the striding child. But then we see that much of this sense is in the figure of the child itself with the uplifted wings of the rain cape, the little hands black against the dark sky, and the shadowy face which tells us nothing....

The beginning of the group which I have called "masquerades" is the Rose Festival Series (1950-53). In *Self Portrait as a Royal Rosarian* the head and the inside of the parasol are sanguine with the most vivid cadmium reds, roses appear on the cheeks, the handle of the parasol has sprouted a tribute of leaves – yet the face looks out under the conventional Rosarian straw, with such somberness it gives the fiery reds a more sinister symbolism. Later...a certain "frothy" treatment of the surface, and the deceptive air of gaiety, will appear again in such paintings as *Voyage of the Neon Horse*, *Fountain of Youth*.... The originality of these works lies in the topical and frequently festive themes he employs for (his) expressive purpose, and in the vitality of a style which changes without hesitation as the artist's intention develops....

Rachael Griffin and Barbara McLarty viewing "The Mountain Show" organized by Image Gallery for Timberline Lodge, August 1962

RACHAEL GRIFFIN, CURATOR, PORTLAND ART MUSEUM
Lecture delivered to the American Association for Aesthetics, Northwest Division, April 1961

This cannot presume to be an iconographic study of the work of McLarty. It is rather a suggestion that much modern work can and should be looked at in this way – especially the work of McLarty.

Embattled schools of art have been the norm in the western world, the factions usually agreeing only on one thing, that is to leave pallid relativism or any other position short of total commitment to the pedants – Museum people, aestheticians and such. But for some years, as we all know, the non-objective artists have drawn even these in their wake, and respectable opinion in the art world has been overwhelmingly of the view that...non-objective art was the art which best expressed our age – that figurative art was a retrogressive horse-and-buggy art.

During those years the voices raised in America in protest against this position were generally weak and unconvincing. Inevitably they attracted...the unspeakable anti-art people who deal in communist plots. Except for these voices, either weak or shrill, there was generally silence. Then David Parks, Diebenkorn, and Bischoff...went figurative together with considerable fanfare; the MOMA exhibition of New Images of Man...supported this slender breach with heavy armor; Canaday and Selden Rodman rushed manuscripts to the presses and something like normalcy was restored with the usual excesses on both sides.

Obviously the most important gain from this adjustment in the art scene has been that attention was drawn to those painters who had been using the figure (and other images from the visual world) all along; talents which had developed a solid following but who had been officially in a sort of limbo. One thinks of Baskin, Hyman Bloom, Ben Shahn, Rico Lebrun. Other gains were: the broadening of the field of art which was beginning to narrow uncomfortably – an event, especially important to the young artist who now may see a greater number of directions to explore; and a healthier critical atmosphere in which the work of art may be approached more fully as a unique, separate, art object, making a greater variety of relationships to our own time, and to both past and present works of art – instead of just one relationship, that is, to other works of this decade and its predominate style. We can examine the permanent or recurring aspects of figurative art which have almost infinite variety, but which have of late been crudely and inaccurately lumped together as social protest, or illustration, or as "literary." This paper is a glance at aspects of this variety with a special emphasis on the work of Jack McLarty....

Here in an early work, a strikingly distorted street which appears as sinister surely, even to the most innocent eye; a toddler with a whirligig staggers onto this neon-lighted stage; looming in black silhouette in the foreground is a figure with an umbrella, a symbol which will appear often in McLarty's work. Topical elements abound. We might pinpoint the decade from the length of skirts...

This rich and handsome design is often read (In the Air) as an abstraction or a construction making use of flowery, winged elements and expressive, perhaps, of plant growth or flight. But at the heart of this winged configuration, if you have not already found it, is a crone on a bucking horse, in a "ride 'em cowboy" posture. The absurd chiffon of her skirt, the horse's white mane, like a leafy stalk, the rider's bony hand and arm are not identified at once. The viewer, aloft with the crone, looks down on the length of the horse's back. On such fearsome incongruities, gleaned from childhood fears or dislikes (the old woman often appears) and such intriguing topical events as rodeos, are many of McLarty's works composed....

(Among McLarty's influences) we shall find Bosch, of course, Grunewald, some of Goya, Breughel, and Rembrandt, and in our own time, Bacon. It is in the main a Northern tradition which admits the monstrous, multifarious images of the subconscious and which is preoccupied with the wild incongruities that lurk, almost visible, in daily appearances, threatening hourly to present themselves openly and shatter the illusions we live by and the order that holds appearances together, however shakily. Thus this art may be said to have moral implications...Costume and carnival, festival and sport, games and make-believe, are the themes and settings; there are no "normal" daily environments; there are old women and young children; gross unnatural figures. There is little reasoned order, in the sense of a room-space with people placed logically in it. There is instead,...a proliferation of figures brought together partly by free association, and by the aesthetic requirements of the plan and theme...

The Voyage of the Neon Horse...has a straightforward playfulness, the follies and incongruities and excesses which everywhere in it abound are a species of wild make-believe in which one sees – at first anyway – no more than a spirit of all-out carnival...Yet when symbols which have sinister meaning in other works appear here it is impossible not to make other associations. And a fuller perusal of the work will uncover these unsettling combinations of beauty and ugliness, gaiety and madness, innocence and evil, which appear in most McLarty works. The composition is processional and the treatment of the surface rich with curling, flowing, leafy, wavy forms. The artist says that he had in his studio at the time... some fascinating large fig leaves which were dried, curling, hollow, sculptural, and these appeared in most canvases at this period, as here, above the absurd and voluptuous cow... (A detailed look will show) the richness and vigor and inventiveness in the painting itself...

Here an involved rhythm of leaf-like forms is the stern of the boat and cowboy playing the guitar to charming cow, sort of sitting in her lap, in fact. In the center top a leaf-like umbrella is held aloft among clouds which are also white leaves, by a bluish silhouette of a cowboy; the hat of a red horse in intellectual hornrims joins these cloud rhythms. He dances with a plump nude adorned with a belt and tiny cowboy hat on her mass of artificial curls.

Very important is the child figure with candid gaze who is often found in McLarty paintings. Around the child (who may be one of his sons) swirls the mad extravaganza. In his fine cowboy suit he plays his part and watches. You see his face, shadowed by hat brim...

Carnival Indians go along with the boat, one holds a banner in the bow, this one swims in the pink champagne sea which is churned by a coronetted oarsman who rows madly with an eggbeater – a symbol of futility, but also a marvelous surefire clown routine. Here...the handsome boots of the guitar-playing cowboy above which we see the leaf-like chaps. These high-heeled boots appear in other paintings, modified to the high-button shoes associated with the sinister old woman or on detached female legs. Sometimes the leg simply ends in this heel and toe shape in the flesh, the leg seeming to have grown into the shape of the footgear.

Here again...we see the strongly processional structure of the composition. McLarty is much interested in the compositional structure of Masaccio, Piero della Francesca and others and enjoys this aspect of painting; but rejects the detached formal consideration whenever the flow of free associations with their symbolic meanings dictates another design or treatment. That is, he does not force the painting into the known moulds of formal beauty or reassuring composition but lets the urgency of the feeling or meaning, and the associations which develop within it, form the finished canvas. Which may be a way of saying that his own temperament forms it.

Games, like carnival, are used in McLarty works as metaphors for life. Here is one of (his) football paintings. The pitifully blown-up and bedecked star makes his play for the approval of the crowd in *Run Past The Stands*...and (we sense) the debilitating exigencies of a game which is largely showmanship...But perhaps that is going too far – or not far enough. In all the paintings there are levels of meanings and mood, flights of fancy, cadenzas which don't labor the central theme. And there are non-thematic aesthetic preoccupations like the leaves which become clouds, umbrellas, hats in the *Neon Horse* and which played a formative part in its appearance and in the effect on the viewer.

This brief look...is meant to be, in part, a reminder of the still unmined riches the human figure offers the contemporary artist; and of the immense variety of states it can express. I am suggesting also that figurative painting be looked at again for the original insights we may find in the content, and for the successful joining of content with formal elements – not slipped over as if the presence of the subject and the suggested symbolic meanings were a slightly embarrassing accident, or a necessary phase through which the painter is moving on his way to freeing himself from the shackles of subject matter. But most of all I propose that it would be our loss if artists, with the special insights and the powerful visual images at their disposal, ceased to use these to throw light on the human condition and the human spirit. I agree with Picasso that the artist is more than a decorator of apartment house walls.

"Cat Cap" (color woodcut) by Jack McLarty circa 1980

JACK McLARTY: PAINTER AS POET
Jane Van Cleve, Stepping Out Northwest, *Number 14, Summer 1982*

If words were his medium, artist Jack McLarty would be a poet. His complex canvasses are charged with a visual language that is highly distilled, emotional, imagistic, and metaphoric. Attentive viewers will find themselves looking at his paintings very hard, up close and from a distance, to get beyond the first impression of enigma to the later, more profound impression that something deeply felt is being shared.

Because this visual language is dense and individualistic, however, it can seem exotic when in fact it's very familiar. This language is drawn from an intricate amalgam of McLarty's objective perceptions and his interior dreams, based on the world we all share: a social world of city streets, spectator sports, and traffic patterns; a private world of bedrooms and gardens where intimate gestures...can have a perilous poignancy. One theme McLarty has worked for a long time is that nothing is quite what it appears.

"What I try to do in different times is develop a vocabulary in painting images that allows me to say and talk about what I respond to and want to state," said in a mild, soft-spoken voice that belies his intensity, even fierceness, about art as a communicative act.

"Poetry is closer to what I do because of the layers of association and meanings possible. You can gain more time. Poetry allows you dense imagery, overlaps, resonances and double images. I've also been influenced by the great muralists," he adds.

"The language of poems and murals allows a direct representation of ideas and a direct condensation of ideas. Particularly in murals, juxtapositions are important. You can consider three or four happenings at once and still make a total of it. In some ways, murals are very much memories of a time rather than a description. Fantasy and imagination do get involved."

We are standing in McLarty's studio, a small but crowded and richly textured space, full of interesting, often contradictory effects. On the shelves, small press books lean against classics. Toy boats, wooden airplanes, hand-carved dolls and lead soldiers mingle casually with pieces of African and Mexican sculpture. Tacked on the walls are postcards, newspaper photographs, prints by other artists, and rough ideas for work in progress. This hodge podge of stimulants projects a sensibility at once personal and democratic, sophisticated and childlike. Just as relevant to the whole picture are the worn out, old chairs.

"There are different kinds of particular vocabulary that become like a cast of characters in a play setting," McLarty continues. "People like Seurat often rejected a setting where something could happen, but I've chosen that kind of setting. It may be a street scene or a market or a butcher shop. The river has been important," he states, indicating the centrality of this image in a new work, "Willamette Wars," which seems an unconventional cityscape at first glance. Even so, we squirm, recognizing the current and terrible urban prospects, made radical by McLarty's...treatment and made "realistic" by how fully he has imagined what we dimly suspect.

"Willamette Wars" is not a difficult painting: what is difficult is facing what we don't want to see. Block-like city buildings encroach upon a river literally clogged out of movement by surface and underground use/abuse, the present marine traffic overlaying a history of sunken objects and bodies. At the seawall a toy-like ship is armed for war. Two-dimensional angular figures, way out of scale to their context, menace each other with cut-out guns. Brightly striped, these hard-edged people look more like packages or gumwrappers than human beings. Not only are the streets crowded, but from out of the sky comes an ambiguous vehicle reminiscent of light rail and "Star Wars." Meanwhile, the tone of the painting is disturbing: the muted blues, yellows, and brown of a gathered weather just before the storm.

On one level, "Willamette Wars" confronts us with the specter of a city sinking under the oppressive struggle of a military-industrial-materialistic investment. But, on another level, the painting is fascinating and beautiful the way a fairy tale illustration is fascinating and beautiful for its riddles, hidden stories, and dramatic balancing of good and evil possibilities.

The landscape behind the city, the hills, resemble the heads of spectators who are not quite involved in Armageddon. The "head" image is echoed in a foreground disk with a glowing serrated edge, suggestive of a sunburst, a coin, or even a ferris wheel.

"An awful lot of what I do has the quality of daydreams," McLarty continues. "And, as soon as you open yourself to images that can be taken as one thing or another deliberately, you allow interpretation, and the viewer can bring his or her own reference to the painting. One of the things people often (fail) to do is to bring their own references to the painting."

"Viewers have to make an effort to actually look and say, 'What is it?' One of the difficulties or disappointments for me is that people don't try to understand what I have gone to a lot of trouble to communicate to them..."

"My experience over a long period of time has been that adults have all these preconceptions about art and, as a result, have difficulty with my paintings, but children invariably like them." He shrugs. "There are all kinds of things going on, and children simply look at them. The fantasy aspects don't bother them at all. They're open to puzzles. They can identify with forms, not literal forms, but imaginative forms."

Lately a new character has entered (McLarty's) universe: a rather pudgy baby with an old-man scowl, busily engaged in breaking his toy – often an airplane or space ship...."I haven't changed my mind about people and that destructive impulse we have," (he) says about a painting that forces us to re-appraise who we are by what we have raised. "I think we find war exciting. I don't think we've resolved these impulses at all."

McLarty's interest in society and how it behaves developed at an early age. When he was two years old, his father, a brick mason, moved the family to a downtown Portland apartment, the first of the small hotels where (he) grew up in close association with neighbors who were lonely, isolated, "some crippled, some lunatic," but also interesting. Instead of being frightened, he identified with these street people and has celebrated them consistently in his work..."There were more individualists at the bottom and at the top than in the middle. Whatever their kick was, they were very open."

Although his interest in art also surfaced early, McLarty had to struggle to find his own path. At Benson High School, he took printing, but at the technological level. He was refused admission to the design classes "because I couldn't letter properly." Then, when he entered the Portland Art Museum School (PNCA) he felt "naive, introverted, shy." He would have dropped out had not Clara Stephens, a faculty artist, urged him to continue.

Another important mentor was William Givler, the eventual dean of the school, who taught McLarty a great deal about painting and composition. "It was composition I connected with, and the whole structure and organization of the painting," says the artist who can still remember school founder, Harry Wentz saying, "For you, art is always going to be a problem to solve."

In 1939 McLarty went to New York, where he studied at the American Artists School and where he first met his long-time friend, painter Louis Bunce. Two important decisions happened at this time, the middle of the Depression, when artists were actively engaged in social, political and aesthetic change. "It's hard to know about your own motivations, but I've always been attached to a social justice theme," says McLarty about his alliance with these reformers and the figurative tradition. "I made up my mind that I wasn't a politician. I'm not that kind of extroverted person, but it's important to me what happens in society and it's what I find I want to talk about all the time."

In New York, McLarty also connected with surrealism as a way to be "pointed" about social issues without being didactic or propagandistic. "I think, when I first encountered surrealism, it had to do with psychology and free association and the double image which was happening with artists like Picasso," McLarty recalls. "At first I didn't understand this viewpoint. I didn't know what was going on. I had to practice to learn to see things that looked like something else. Though I was very poetic, I was very literal-minded. But surrealism touched a chord in me: how one thing could look like something else and could mean, as a result, something quite different than it apparently did."

"I still believe that the general appearance of things and the accepted idea of things is not really what is going on a lot of the time," he says candidly. "Body language and non-verbal communication – those things are fundamental both in conversation and in life. Life is much more complex and much more is going on than you can consciously talk about or analyze."

It was this kind of perspicacity that McLarty brought to his own work upon his return to Portland. "At first I felt lost. I was copying everyone: Picasso, Rouault, Modigliani. Finally I decided to do what I knew best, and I went downtown to the public market and the waterfront. The river is sort of the center of Portland. At least it has been for me. The idea of the city, the city I live in – the buildings, the slums, Burnside, the theater – is the kind of world that has always concerned me directly."

McLarty began teaching at the Museum Art School. He and his wife Barbara started their family, and in the available time he explored the deeper implications of seemingly ordinary subject matter. A natural ironist, he would notice the very bright dresses worn by grim-faced senior citizens. He would see the absurdity of a fire hydrant spewing water in front of a flaming building. In one portrait of a butcher… (he) made an heroic case not only for the worker, but for the meat: he was interested in the look of fat, the color of internal flesh, the beautiful form of a shank or an apron or a chopping block.

Following his own hunches and "free associations," what he didn't worry about was commercial success. "Some people (artists) sensed a little bit what people would respond to or how much they would pay, but I really wasn't that practical. During the first fifteen years, I sold just three paintings, and there wasn't any expectation of making a living by painting," he says about these formative years.

"Every artist in that period knew he had to do something else. In this country poets and artists have had to finance their own freedom. What you have is the option, if you're willing to pay for it, to do whatever you want. You can express yourself, you can say anything you want, but you may have to pay for it if this expression isn't acceptable to the general public…"

"Even though I arbitrarily think that I am painting for people – I don't want to be an elitist at all, I want painting to be just a common thing – I think that the distortion and sentimentalizing and gimmicky things that I don't want to do are what made a Disney successful, for example."

"But a lot of people who sell a lot better than I do are people who simply don't touch on any kind of deeper or more pointed aspects of society. They keep their work very superficial and safe and pretty much on the picture postcard level. It's sometimes better than that, but it doesn't really probe more deeply than that the actual meaning of life…"

"I've also avoided using obvious skill," McLarty continues. "At the time that I had to give up Norman Rockwell, that kind of aesthetic, I realized that I really disliked painting and art that seduces people by its skill. But, if you don't want that association with skill, you have to replace it with a more intuitive or emotional track. You have to force yourself to other choices."

"For example, I love color. I love color beautiful, but I will also explore color as an irritant. I really like decorative patterning, but I don't want a decorative quality in my painting. I have always been just mad about the juxtaposition of something beautiful and something terrible," he grins.

"Football uniforms, even when what football players do can be violent."

In the darkened living room, the slide projector hums, flashing image after image that speaks to McLarty's articulateness as a painter. Often, his spring boards are mundane – the football game, the rainy day…but the transformations become wondrous as a single image takes on its own life and gathers momentum from canvas to canvas. What is also amazing is that one man could have originated so much color, such a variety of effects, drawing from all kinds of visual traditions to shape a viewpoint at once imaginative and full of common sense.

"Sometimes I will think about a lot of things and not get much done"…(he) doesn't see himself as terribly prolific. "I think you just have to get beyond this point and paint out your preoccupations. Sometimes an image grows on you, and you need more than one or several paintings to explore it. But sometimes you lose your conviction about a theme. Sometimes your images don't die out altogether, but they diminish into a minor role, and sometimes later they'll come back again. It's obvious that certain kinds of things intuitively mean a great deal to you, but others come and go."

We are looking at a "running athlete," a McLarty character of many years' standing, who, on this canvas, is running pell-mell toward the edge of the playing field, which becomes the edge of the globe. In a subtle way, this figure precurses the hill-heads, so bubble-like in "Willamette Wars." But in the '60s the "running athlete" has evolved into a fat baroque cherub about to sprout wings in an airborne leap through a light-streaked heavenly sky.

"The streaking is a device that is obvious in a sense," says McLarty, "but as soon as you start adapting it, you absorb it in your own way. With me, the streaking did a number of things. For example, I started associating it with light and rain, and then it became spatial. By putting streaks ahead and behind, I found I could contain images differently. It was a formal device part of the time. Then, by staining the canvas with streaks and leaving trailings of light, I could really get the effect of light, which has always interested me. You see, some of the light is untouched canvas, which gives off a quality quite different from light streaks painted on."

The rendering of the athlete, too, seems more energy than form. This figure is at once clumsy and buoyant, at once a clod and a dancer. Although McLarty has used photographs of players running or jumping, cut from the sport pages of newspapers, he will change the direction of the figure or work out of his observations of ballet and movement to catch the emotion of the athlete. "Sport photographs always emphasize frozen action experience, not the feeling of the experience," he contends. "Those frozen images have nothing to do with the blurred smack impact of the physical experience."

At the same time, McLarty is clearly interested in metamorphosis, whereby the running athlete is not one individual, but an archetype that can manifest creative freedom in one guise, social conformity in another. As much as he is a genuine fan of football games, golf matches, wrestling matches, rodeos, and pinball machines, McLarty sees in all gaming activities the essential conflicts between civilized and brute impulses.

"That kind of figure, the running athlete, is like a Crucifixion image," he explains. "It's not meant to represent a man. It's meant to represent a whole range of ideas and emotional attitudes. In order to have that complexity of association, the figure cannot be realistic. It has to be symbolic or suggestive."

"And the stripes and patterns of his uniform have always been related in my mind to other patterns in life of all kinds: patterns of thinking, patterns of social behavior – like contrails and construction pipes in buildings that are half-built. When you see the guts of the building and the veins and intestinal system of a building when it is unfinished, in some ways the whole composition can become a big figure."

How much do we "create" our world? How much does our world re-create us? This question has preoccupied McLarty in recent canvasses, where he has explored the human aspects of machines and the machine aspects of human beings. In this strand of work, the shapes will be very simple and definite; the whole painting by its specificity will evoke the innocence and directness of children's drawings. A city full of cars. A bus at a crossroads. "Well, I guess I think all those things – cars and clothes and other manmade shapes are designed like human beings and so often have that appearance."

"You find yourself thinking, 'Well, maybe it's a functional machine, but why does it have two eyes and a mouth and so on?' Very fundamentally, I think people who design are influenced by body structure." In other words, the tank with a face, the helicopter that looks like a wasp, get neutralized out of violent implications by their formal familiarity…

It's the democracy of McLarty regarding subject matter

and his curiosity about a painter's means (light, color, shape, texture, tone and composition) that makes his work so rangy. On a small scale, he can paint a still life of roses, for example …and strike a chord of recognition for that moment when the deep reds become blue, the color evacuates form, and flowers that were alive enter another state, exquisitely poignant and beautiful….

(Doing) 'social issue' canvasses, he often uses humor to underscore 'hidden' aspects of public commitments. In "A Big Red One," for example, the central image is ambiguously a rocket, a bus, a phallus, constructed entirely of cars….

As a teacher and artist, he has influenced at least two generations of colleagues and students, who will often incorporate McLartyesque 'imagery' into their own work. "It is interesting that this happens, and I think it's good," (he) says modestly about his impact on the local art community. "Almost any group of artists can seem like a school even through they eventually develop in different directions. Everyone shouldn't be influenced by Picasso or New York. They should be much more convinced about their local contemporaries than they often are. You can't have several hundred thousand artists all looking at the same stuff and reading the same things without an awful lot of formulaic work that is not personal and becomes redundant," he believes.

"You also wish that the art audience would recognize local art work," McLarty continues, restating his conviction that the artist is an ordinary citizen of a particular place, time and tradition, who happens to use visual means to 'make his mark' or 'say his piece' about these circumstances….

"You know people underestimate what they can absorb," he observes. "They don't realize that art, quality art, is really pervasive…in sorting out art and labelling one thing 'minor' and another 'major' (they) try to say there are very few good things, not realizing the fact they're just trying to simplify their lives."

McLarty is smiling mischievously. It's the mischief in McLarty you learn to watch as well as his compassionate empathy. In fact, a large part of his work has been about what we leave out, choosing a language of convenience. Through often outrageous imagery and his own fantasy worlds, McLarty will expose the fallacies of our fantasy worlds, and his art becomes a counterpoint to our artfulness, 'seeing' only what we want to believe.

NORTHWEST VIEWPOINTS – JACK McLARTY
January 6-28, 1988
Portland Art Museum
John S. Weber, Adjunct Curator

Over the last five years Jack McLarty has added a new chapter to a forty year career as one of Oregon's leading artists. Populated by giant babies, colorful robots, fantastic toys and buildings, McLarty's recent paintings erupt with visionary dismay at the state of human society. His scenes of Portland's Willamette River waterfront show a surreal city overrun by outlandish creatures, while his pictures of oversized babies feature nightmare infants clutching with greedy abandon at anything within reach. Throughout this work, McLarty mixes a ribald carnival atmosphere with social commentary to create a provocative view of late-century American civilization. Jocular and welcoming at first glance, McLarty's paintings reveal themselves as edgy, disturbing, and peculiarly complex upon longer acquaintance.

McLarty grew up during the politically volatile years of the Great Depression, and social awareness has consistently influenced his artmaking. In the 1980s, McLarty's work seems to acquire an added bite, as if in response to the polarized, often paralyzed political climate of the decade. But it would be both impossible and inappropriate to pigeonhole McLarty as primarily a "political artist," for his painting reaches simultaneously in a variety of thematic and emotional directions. McLarty's work is informed as much by his abiding interest in art history as by political conscience, and he is influenced as well by folk art, popular culture, and design. The artist blends these sources in an original body of images which bear the distinct stamp of his time, place, and personality.

In "The East Side as the Garden of Eden," McLarty, a lifelong Portlander, looks out across his homeland and sees not an Oregon Eden, but Portland as a twentieth-century paradise lost. Mount Hood appears directly in the center of the canvas – a distant, picturesque peak. But between the west hills and the mountain, high-rise buildings and freeways dominate the riverscape. To the north, Mount St. Helens pours a cloud of black ash into the sky. The downtown district lies in the shadow, pockmarked by craters. On the East Side, monstrous, wildly colored creatures cavort among recognizable landmarks of the city – while a huge pig sits (approximately in the location of Lloyd Center) and stares dumbly at the monolithic form of the U.S. Bank Tower. In the far background, a cherubic pair of babies marches arm-in-arm away from the city, while two American Indians peer from behind Mount Hood at the state's largest city. Portland architectural and cultural institutions such as the Union Station, Oaks Park, the Washington Park Zoo (represented by an elephant) and Corno's Grocery also appear.

"The East Side as the Garden of Eden" is McLarty's biting celebration of a Portland he sees behind the city's chamber-of-commerce facade – a Portland of chaos, passion, excess, and lost innocence. McLarty's painting is raw…his palette garish and hot. His images, humorous and barbed, depart radically from the Oregon of popular imagination; the green home of lumberjacks and backpackers. Avoiding a literal depiction of the city, he has recast city and landscape painting to create a domain of fantasy and ironic social history. As much as anything, this work is a phantasmagoric "history-scape" in which McLarty muses ruefully on civilization's encroachment upon what was once, indeed, a wild paradise. Although numerous landmarks situate the image clearly in the present, McLarty's polemical view of Portland clearly challenges his local viewers to think about their city in historical terms, to ask what Portland has been and where it may be headed.

(His) other recent forays into landscape, including "Willamette Wars," "Giant in Trouble,"…possess the same hybrid character as "The East Side" without offering its wealth of specific historical references. In these pictures McLarty invents a population of imaginary beings situated in an equally imaginary geography. But if the multicolored stick-men, robots, toys, boats, and creatures of "Willamette Wars" are no more real in literal terms than the balloony hills fronting the river, both serve to express (his) sense of the emotional reality of the Portland waterfront. It is a world of frantic activity and aggression, populated by colorful but threatening characters. Everything is brightly decorated, yet shoddy and shallow – a world of cookie-cutouts and cardboard zombies masquerading as living beings. In the background exquisitely patterned hills, peculiar spheroids, and hovering UFOs seem about to come crashing down on the city itself, represented by an anonymous row of flag-flying skyscrapers. Like so much of (his) work (it) is a compelling mixture of reckless energy and troubling undercurrents.

"Giant in Trouble"…echo(es) the mood of raucous unease found in "Willamette Wars." In the former, a city skyline can be seen emblazoned across the torso of a giant beset by a braying menagerie of weird animals. The giant stands knee-deep in a river filled with wreckage on one side and a steamship on the other. Mount Hood appears once again in the distance. Planes crash to the ground and a female figure seems to plummet to the earth, perhaps in a metaphoric reference to the city's fall from grace. Here again, everything is lively and bright but precariously out of balance.

…McLarty brings yet another figure into the landscape: the mammoth infant which assumes an increasing role in the more recent paintings. The baby varies with each incarnation, but always it appears overweight and malevolent…by "Red Baby" it has overwhelmed virtually all else in the picture. Always, the baby is consumed by its own activity, which usually consists of torturing or tearing apart one of the robotic stick-men or flimsy machines sharing its world. In turn, the toys strike back by firing pistols, sticking the baby with swords or dive-bombing it from the air. Yet nothing seems to have an effect. Indeed, the child concentrates on its destructive play as only an infant can, unaware of the furor around it….

As a group the babies are clearly McLarty's way of pointing out that humankind has grown larger without reaching maturity. Able to concentrate only on small, selfish acts of mayhem, the overgrown child remains largely unaware of the world around it. Everything appears to the infant as a gimcrack toy suited only for immediate play and pleasure. The baby's toys have grown bigger and now threaten to overwhelm their nominal master. But nothing here is substantial or built to last: depth exists in this world solely in the form of the baby's corpulence, and its toys are just cardboard boxes covered with jazzy wrapping paper….

"Children of the Mind" offers yet another reflection on self-portraiture, as McLarty places himself in the midst of the cutout figures, animals, machines, babies, and cars which have inhabited his art for more than a decade. The effect is like a class reunion in a surrealist toy factory. (His) inscrutable face peers out from the middle of his army of creations; humorous elements clash with an overall sense of militaristic, automated mayhem. In the foreground, a battleship on wheels aims its cannons out at the viewer. He implies that his creatures are children of his own mind, just as the real machines which populate the real world are children of humanity.

In terms of method, Jack McLarty's art reflects influences synthesized from a variety of sources. His use of bright, out-of-the-tube colors reveals the artist's enthusiasm for Fauve coloration and the unabashed brilliance of much Mexican folk art. His flying machines and curious, boxy figures seem related to early twentieth-century Cubo-Futurist styles, and the frenetic activity depicted in his work echoes the Futurists' fascination with velocity. But where the Futurists expressed an aggressive optimism about machines and speed, McLarty – with the wisdom of a post-Hiroshima perspective – shows a world of machines gone mad.

Despite this fast pace, the mood in McLarty's images often seems dreamlike, and the artist credits Surrealism for his metaphoric, free-associational approach to representation and form. Through its exploration of dreams and the unconscious mind, Surrealism taught (him) that fantasy is often more real than "reality"; furthermore, Surrealism showed that art, through invention and imagination, could begin to tap an underlying world which the rational, conscious mind often repressed.

Other twentieth-century influences include the great Mexican muralists Diego Rivera and Jose Clemente Orozco, as well as Max Beckmann of Germany. Rivera and Orozco bequeathed compositions overflowing with vitality, as well as a commitment to imaginative and politically engaged history painting. As for Beckmann, his ability to create a metaphorically powerful vocabulary of images is a model for McLarty's own method. Peter Breughel and Hieronymus Bosch, the two great Flemish painters of the Northern Renaissance, provide yet an earlier precedent for (his) use of landscape as an arena for social commentary. More specifically, his "East Side as the Garden of Eden" – a broad stretch of land viewed from on high, populated by surrealistic, often out-of-scale creatures – is in form and content a twentieth-century update of one of Bosch's favored motifs: landscape as moral fable.

Like Beckmann, Bosch, Breughel, Rivera and Orozco, McLarty thrives on dualities which reflect all sides of life: horror and beauty, ecstasy and dismay, intense color and dark humor. Like all five, he loads each picture with as many figures and as much activity as possible, juxtaposing idea against idea and piling image upon image. McLarty counts on, indeed, demands the viewer's active willingness to unravel this work, for contrasting elements and dichotomies prevail. Fantasy and imagination are the only guide(s).

In view of the diverse sources of McLarty's work, it is intriguing to examine him as a "regional artist." Born in 1919 in Seattle, he was raised on the Portland waterfront above the Hawthorne Bridge and studied at the Museum Art School. After a stay of two years in New York City, he returned to Portland, where he has been an active participant in the local art scene since the mid-1940s. As an artist, a teacher in the Museum Art School, and a founder of the Image Gallery, with his wife, Barbara, (he) has influenced more than one generation of Oregon artists. His work, as is clear in this exhibition, often deals openly, if critically, with regional themes. Yet in another sense, McLarty's work reveals the inadequacy of the term and makes it clear that the historical conditions of "regionalism" have undergone a major transformation in the 1980s.

In the period between the World Wars, self-avowed regionalists such as Thomas Hart Benton argued for an American painting which rejected "international" European styles to concentrate on depictions of the American scene …the term "regional artist" gradually came to mean anyone who didn't live, work, and show in New York. Today, New York remains the major marketplace for world art. But the rise of postmodernism in the 1980s has ushered in a variety of retooled versions of early twentieth-century art movements and thereby allowed a reassessment of artists who, for example, never abandoned figurative painting. Art…does not appear to be moving in any single, dominant historical direction, freeing artists to work in a great variety of manners…

To Jack McLarty – who admits to wondering in the late 1950s and 1960s if it still made sense to paint figures and landscape – the 1980s have meant that his art can now be seen in a context broader than that of the most recent New York styles. This is a welcome development, for (he) represents the best tradition of regionalism: artists working where they live and responding to their environment critically and imaginatively, making the work they feel must be made, and yet fully aware of the wider history of art.

1. *Portland* (oil) 1943 24 x 18

2. *The Orange Umbrella* (oil) 1944 41½ x 24

Visitors to Reed College faculty lounge this month have an opportunity to study the work of one of Oregon's very capable painters and teachers – Jack McLarty. Reed is giving (him) a One-Man show, an honor well deserved by this President of Artists Equity, Oregon Chapter.

We visited the Artist in the attic studio of his home and then went to Reed to study the exhibition. What we saw was the visual experience of the thinking of this young man...and it is about the Portland he knows that he is chiefly concerned in drawings and paintings. His boyhood was spent in the vicinity of the (old) Farmers' Market (SW Yamhill Street) and he is still studying the color and designs of market stalls, the people who frequent the area and those who sell there...

McLarty gets close to the spirit of events and places which are a part of Portland. And pinned up on his studio wall, between drawings are numerous newspaper photographic clippings of the Rose Festival and other events. He always attends the parades "to get some notes"... but the exact-instant prints by news photographers are (also) used as idea suggestions. One painting made from a sketch hastily done in the market area is of an old woman who wore a flower-covered hat, and a flower-design handbag and was carrying flowers in a shopping bag...

Louise Aaron, Art Editor, *The Oregon Journal*, February 1953.

3. *Self-Portrait with the River* (oil) 1945 12 x 26

4. *Night City with Nude* (oil) 1946 32 x 43

Portland Scenes are featured in the paintings of Jack McLarty in the Oregon Guild Gallery (Portland Art Museum). Artist McLarty has a gift for portraying the life of his community and the personalities of the people who live there. His subjects are never just a collection of buildings, the interiors of rooms, or an interesting street. His architectural features, bold as they are, are merely the settings for the human drama which is sensed rather than staged pictorially...

Catherine Jones, *The Oregonian,* April 1948.

5. *Waterfront* (oil) 1946 32 x 43

We just finished addressing and bundling 1390 McLarty announcements and I am taking them and this to the post office post haste....

The installation of your work went in a different direction than I had preconceived...less essay and more a beautiful moving formal painting and drawing exhibition...it is very much a joy to light your painting...I never realized just how sensitive and important a surface is there, until I got them on my walls (at Bush House) and started throwing lights at them...anyway, on Sunday you will see my sins...

personal letter to the Artist from **Jack Eyerly,** *Director, Bush House Museum, Salem, Oregon, May 31, 1961.*

What a wonderful day we had last Thursday! I'm so glad you urged me to come for Jack's exhibition – to see how great he is – that sort of show arranging the paintings in order of time is a fine way to do it.

The ones with all kinds of subjects were most impressive to me – like *Fountain of Youth and Neon Horse*...a combination of good plays, novels, poems, essays in paint – as he puts there the world of people. You just can't see everything or any part of the things he is telling us when you have only a few hours to look, or days or weeks probably. But what an exciting thing it is to meet an artist on a canvas like those. The next morning I wanted to go back for another day, perhaps by myself, and look again (like books and poetry in which you find more and more).

personal letter to **Barbara McLarty** *from* **Jane Huston Rawlins** *about McLarty Show in The Dalles, October 1961.*

6. *City Song* (oil) 1946 36 x 18

7. *City on Fire* (oil) 1947 32 x 43

8. *Sub-Portland* (oil) 1947 24 x 36

9. *Conflagration Point* (oil) 1948-49 43 x 32

10. *Parade Watchers* (oil) 1949 36 x 29

11. *Barbara and Polly with a Book* (oil) 1950 43 x 32

12. *Rose Parade* (oil) c. 1952 44 x 72

13. *King of the River* (oil) 1951 36 x 18

14. *Old Woman with Flowers* (oil) c. 1952 40 x 20

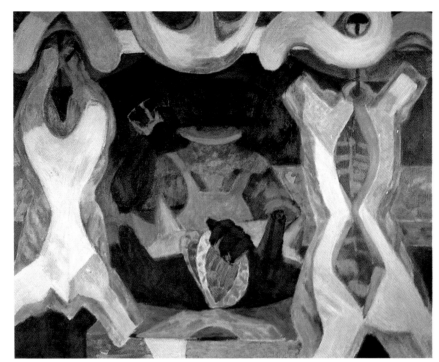

15. *The Butcher Shop* (oil) c. 1952 44½ x 36

16. *Self-Portrait as a Royal Rosarian* (oil) 1951 24 x 30

DEACCESSIONED

SAINT LOUIS ART MUSEUM LIBRARY

17. *Tall Self-Portrait in Blue* (oil) c. 1953
42 x 24

18. *Family Portrait* (oil) 1953 32 x 45

Content is of paramount importance in the work of Jack McLarty. He has a sharp awareness of our life condition, and traditional and modern art movements have been assimilated into a highly personal idiom....Since I started collecting McLarty's work twenty years ago, the work has shown a consistency in style and a true mastery of materials....The complexities of the compositions reveal ideas that have been deliberately hidden in forms and colors...revealed to us only after much looking so (they) become meaningful to own. The complexities of the world are within the work, and the visual interpretations are completely controlled. The artist's view of life is camouflaged in rainbows of color and imaginatively complex forms... It is an enduring art, a history of our time, the visual response of a genuine artist.

Lillie H. Lauha, March 10, 1972.

19. *A Child's World* (oil) 1955 42 x 32

1919   Born in Seattle to Sophia Amelia (Jensen) and George McLarty. Christened William James, he is immediately called Jack, the professional name he has always used. His father, a stonemason/brickmason, soon has problems when his building trade falls off drastically. His mother, ever resourceful, gets into the restaurant business on a small scale, supporting the family during bad times. (In an interview with Julia Ruuttila in November 1980, on her 100th birthday, she proudly stated that she still retained her membership in Local #9, the Hotelworkers Union.)

1921   Family moves to Portland. They are to run at least three different small hotels for working class people over the next thirty years. Last of these was the Dently Hotel, 1212 S.W. 4th, across from the City Hall in a block now converted to a park.

1925   Enters First Grade at the Ladd School, located on the site of the present Pacific Northwest College of Art. Later he attends Shattuck, following the demolition of Ladd School and construction of the Portland Art Museum on the Park Blocks.

1933   Enrolls at Benson Polytechnic High School where he studies Vocational Printing (Typography) and plays baseball. He says that working on the linotype greatly improved his spelling. Following graduation in June 1937 he signs up for classes at the Advertising Art School, a long-time fixture in downtown Portland. He finds the instruction unsatisfactory and quits very shortly.

1937   In the fall he enrolls in classes at the Museum Art School, attending half-time and helping his parents in the Dently part-time. He finds himself quite unprepared for the relative sophistication of both students and classes and quits midway through his first year. It is a turning point for him. Only the kind and sensitive encouragement of Clara Jane Stephens, one of his instructors, causes him to return to the school. She urges him to continue, stressing her belief in his talent.

1939   Receives 2nd Place in the annual Carey Drawing Prize Competition. 1st Place is won by Josh Taylor who will become Director of the National Collection of Fine Arts, Smithsonian Institution.

1940   He goes to New York. He studies first with Sol Wilson at the American Artists School. Then he works with Anton Refregier, the noted muralist. Finally, he studies with Joe Solman, with whom he finds he has great rapport. He is much affected by Solman, both by his attitude and by the street scenes he is painting at that time. This is a very lonely period for him, especially the first year. Then he connects with Eda and Louis Bunce. He rents a room from them, and he enters the circle of their friends from Oregon who are living in New York, and this includes Fred and Dorothy Farr and Alton Pickens.

1942 Returns to Portland after deciding that New York does not suit him for a long-term home. He rents studio space near the river and the bridges and begins to help around the Dently Hotel again. Returning to his old haunts in the downtown, he begins to draw and paint the streets and buildings, the market stalls, the news vendors that are so familiar to him. Begins work as an electrician's helper in the shipyards, on a night shift.

1944 "Portland" (oil) shown at San Francisco Art Institute.

1945 Executes a mural at Laurelhurst School, funded by the PTA for the library. It is a memorial to veterans who died in World War II and is based on favorite characters from books, selected in a poll of the students.

Accepts a teaching-fellowship in Lithography at the Museum Art School, Working with his long-time mentor and friend, Bill Givler, he will produce all of the work he will do in this print medium, during the year that follows.

Executes a mural at Collins View School based on characters from fairytales. A favorite aunt, Alice Blair, is teaching at the school and she encourages this project, which is funded by the PTA.

Holds his first one-man show, in the Oregon Guild Gallery, Portland Art Museum. He sells one painting, to Abraham Maslow, who is visiting Portland. The subject is of an old woman.

1946 "War Years" (oil) receives Honorable Mention, 32nd Annual Exhibition of Northwest Artists, Seattle Art Museum. It goes on circuit in Washington State.

Fourth All-Oregon Exhibition, Portland Art Museum.

"The City" (oil) is shown in 1st Annual Pasadena National Exhibition, Pasadena Museum. C.S. Price is the only other Oregon painter included.

Is married in August in McMinnville to Barbara Lever, a graduate of Linfield College who has been working at the Museum on the recommendation of Catherine Jones of the Oregonian. Katie always took credit for arranging this match.

1947 Joins the teaching staff of the Museum Art School, as part-time instructor.

"War Years" is chosen by both regional and national juries for Paintings of the Year, a traveling exhibition sponsored by Pepsi-Cola.

1948 One-man Show in the Oregon Guild Gallery, Portland Art Museum.

Starts "Newport School of Art" with Louis Bunce. They offer outdoor painting/drawing classes for 6 weeks. Headquarters are the old Abbey Hotel on Yaquina Bay and at Nye Beach. Evolved this to cover summer expenses when teachers were paid only during the school year. The summer classes continue for two years.

1949 First child, a daughter is born in May, Polly Harrison.

"Social Dimension" (oil) receives top Purchase Prize at the 35th Annual Exhibition of Northwest Artists, Seattle Art Museum.

1951 One-man Show in Oregon Artists Gallery, Portland Art Museum.

One-man Show at Kharouba Gallery, a fine professional outlet run by Eda and Louis Bunce, Portland.

Artists of Oregon 1951, Portland Art Museum.

1952 Pacific Arts Festival, Oakland Museum.

Artists of Oregon 1952, Portland Art Museum.

Prints by Oregon Artists 1952, Portland Art Museum.

Executes a mural at Riverdale School based on Greek mythology.

Takes a summer trip by train to New York to visit galleries and museums.

1953 Artists of Oregon 1953, Portland Art Museum.

One-man Show Kharouba Gallery, Portland.

39th Annual Exhibition of NW Artists, Seattle Art Museum.

First son is born in June, Hugh Jensen.

Is now working with serigraph process in printmaking.

1954 Artists of Oregon 1954, Portland Art Museum.

40th Annual Exhibition of NW Artists, Seattle Art Museum.

Special Citation from Museum of Modern Art, New York, for Play Sculpture Competition. His design: a double climbing wall.

1955 "The Shop" (woodcut) receives Honorable Mention 7th Oregon Annual Print Exhibition, Portland Art Museum.

41st Annual Exhibition of NW Artists, Seattle Art Museum.

Second son is born in March, Charles Malcolm.

1956 Artists of Oregon 1956: Drawings and Prints, Portland Art Museum.

Daughter Polly dies after a 3 year illness. The family is profoundly affected. References are found in the work throughout the period 1953-1960.

Gives "The Seasons" (triptych) to Multnomah County Library for the Children's Room in memory of Polly.

42nd Annual Exhibition of NW Artists, Seattle Art Museum.

1957 One-man Show Portland Art Museum. "Persephone" (oil) is recommended for purchase. They do not buy it; however, a private collector, Jan Mauritz, does and presents it to the Museum under the donor program.

A second daughter is born in January, Laura Marguerite.

Is invited to show in 2nd Pacific Coast Biennial of Paintings/ Watercolors, Santa Barbara Museum. Show circulates to Calif. Palace of Legion of Honor, San Francisco; Seattle Art Museum; Portland Art Museum.

One-man Show at Bush House Museum, Salem, Oregon.

Father dies suddenly of a heart attack at age 81.

1958 Northwest Printmakers Annual Exhibition, Henry Gallery, University of Washington, Seattle.

Artists of Oregon 1958, Portland Art Museum.

Participates in 4-man painting show at Artists' Gallery, Seattle, run by James Fitzgerald/Margaret Tompkins. The other painters: Louis Bunce, Byron Gardner and Don Sorensen.

Serves on Arts & Decorations Committee, Portland Zoological Society.

Chairman, Artist Membership, Portland Art Association.

Moderates forum, "Art in Architecture," and presents special award to Walter Gordon.

Undertakes brief teaching job at Tucker-Maxon School.

Is invited to 1st Annual Invitational for Drawings & Prints, University of Portland.

1959 "Water Sports" (oil) wins award in Oregon Scene Show, Oregon Centennial Exposition. Purchased by Lillie Lauha and offered to Portland Art Museum under donor program.

Group Exhibition, Ruthermore Galleries, San Francisco.

Exhibits jointly with George Johanson at College of Puget Sound, Tacoma.

Designs play sculpture for Wood Products Pavilion, Oregon Centennial Exposition.

"Spectre of the West" (oil) is reproduced in color in Northwest Review, University of Oregon, Centennial Issue.

Paintings and Sculpture of the Pacific Northwest: Oregon, Washington, British Columbia, Portland Art Museum. Show circulates to Seattle and Vancouver, B.C.

Serves as Acting Dean, Museum Art School, Portland.

50th Anniversary Exhibition of Museum Art School Faculty, Portland Art Museum.

Lectures on Van Gogh during Van Gogh Exhibition, Portland Art Museum.

1960 One-man Show of Paintings and Drawings, Reed College, Portland.

Artists of Oregon 1960, Portland Art Museum.

46th Annual Exhibition of Northwest Artists, Seattle Art Museum.

Northwest Review Fall Issue, University of Oregon, features "The Metaphorical Art of Jack McLarty" by Rachael Griffin, Curator of Portland Art Museum.

1961 One-man Show, Ruthermore Galleries, San Francisco.

47th Annual Exhibition of NW Artists, Seattle Art Museum.

Northwest Painters 1961, invitational for Oregon, Washington, British Columbia, University of Oregon Museum, Eugene.

One-man Show, Bush House Museum, Salem, Oregon.

Coordinates the "Dada Show" in Portland. This was a serious, cooperative effort involving most of the professional artists and art students of the area, as well as Reed College musicians and composers. It was a response to, and an attempt to, link the Dada movement to the emergent "Pop Art" movement of New York, which did not yet have a label.

Opens the Image Gallery with wife, Barbara, at 2483 Northwest Overton, Portland. Attempting to revitalize the languishing gallery scene, some 19 professional artists and 22 collectors contribute to the cost of the start-up. Fred Rudat designs and helps to build the gallery installation.

1962 One-man Show of 30 Drawings, Salt Lake Art Center.

Is invited to show in Pacific Coast Invitational, Fine Arts Gallery of San Diego. Show circulates during 1963 to: Santa Barbara Museum of Art; Municipal Gallery of Los Angeles; San Francisco Museum of Art; Seattle Art Museum; Portland Art Museum.

"Race for Space" (oil) receives Special Mention, Artists of Oregon 1962, Portland Art Museum.

"Hunter at Noon" (oil) is selected for Museum of Modern Art, Recent Painting USA: The Figure. Only other Oregon painter included is James McGarrell.

"Take-off" (drawing) wins Purchase Award, Oregon Art Annual, Erb Memorial Union, University of Oregon, Eugene.

One-man Show, Image Gallery, Portland.

"Self-Portrait" (oil) is shown in 15th Annual Spokane-Pacific Northwest Exhibition, Cheney-Cowles Museum, Spokane.

Tacoma Arts League Invitational.

"World Jumper" (oil) is chosen for Northwest Art Today, Seattle World's Fair.

The McLartys organize and hang a large and impressive show of paintings and sculpture in August at Timberline Lodge at the request of Richard Kohnstamm. They call it "The Mountain Show" and attendance and public response is gratifying. The Lodge purchases an outstanding Percy Manser painting from the show; it portrays mountain climbers and it is later stolen from the Lodge.

1963   20 year Retrospective of Paintings and Drawings, Portland Art Museum. Catalog with Introduction by Francis J. Newton; text by Rachael Griffin.

19th Artists West of the Mississippi: the Realistic Image, Colorado Springs Fine Arts Center.

Pacific Northwest Art, the Haseltine Collection, University of Oregon Museum, Eugene.

49th Annual Exhibition of Northwest Artists, Seattle Art Museum.

One-man Show, Pacific University, Forest Grove, Oregon.

Juries 2nd Annual Christmas Art Show, State Capitol Museum, Olympia, Washington.

Artists of Oregon 1963, Portland Art Museum.

1964   Governor's Invitational for Oregon Artists, State Capitol Museum, Olympia.

35th Printmakers International, Seattle Art Museum and Portland Art Museum.

"The Black Coat" (aquatint) chosen for 1st International Miniature Print Exhibition, Pratt Graphic Art Center, New York, a traveling show.

One-man Show, Woodside Gallery, Seattle.

4th Pacific Northwest Art Annual, Invitational Print Exhibition, Erb Memorial Union, University of Oregon.

Juries the Lakeside Artists Eighth Annual Exhibition, Tacoma.

One-man Show, Linfield College, McMinnville, Oregon.

Takes sabbatical leave from Museum Art School to spend summer in Europe traveling with Barbara. They visit France,

Italy. She returns to open Image Gallery for fall; he visits Switzerland, Holland, makes prints in Paris.

1965   51st Annual Exhibition of Northwest Artists, Seattle Art Museum.

"Over the Edge" (oil) reaches the finals in 29th Corcoran Biennial, Corcoran Gallery, Washington, D.C.

"Take-Off in Grey" (oil) receives Best in Show award, 18th Annual Spokane-Pacific Northwest Exhibition, Cheney-Cowles Museum, Spokane.

He and Barbara attend the gala weekend opening of Salishan Lodge on the Oregon Coast. They will act as consultants to Betty and John Gray, will hang shows for them in the Lodge Gallery, planned as a showcase for the finest Northwest artists.

Printmakers in Oregon Invitational, organized by Ron Tore Janson, Director, at Maude Kerns Art Center, Eugene, it travels to Linfield College, Image Gallery, Salishan Lodge Gallery.

2nd Small Sculpture & Drawing Exhibition, Western Washington State College, Bellingham.

"Teach Me to Fly" (oil) receives Purchase Award, 1st Invitational Exhibition, Lewis and Clark College, Portland.

1966   Twenty Portland Painters, an invitational sponsored jointly by Portland Art Museum and Portland State College in conjunction with annual meeting of the Western Museum Association.

Faculty Exhibition, Museum Art School, Portland Art Museum.

"17 Love Poems" published by Image Gallery. Designed and produced by Clyde Van Cleve with 8 original woodcuts by Jack McLarty. Limited edition of 100 sells out.

Executes a full-page drawing of Bernard Malamud for cover of Northwest Magazine, The Oregonian, Sunday, October 9.

"Circle of Love" (color woodcut) wins Purchase Award, Northwest Printmakers Exhibition, Henry Gallery, University of Washington, Seattle.

"The Woman" (aquatint) chosen for 2nd International Miniature Print Exhibition, Pratt Graphic Art Center, New York, a traveling show.

52nd Annual Exhibition of Northwest Artists, Seattle Art Museum.

Artists of Oregon 1966, Portland Art Museum.

1967   53rd Annual Exhibition of Northwest Artists, Seattle Art Museum.

Artists of Oregon 1967, Portland Art Museum.

One-man Show, Corvallis Art Center.

One-man Show, Image Gallery.

Creates "Emerging Woman" (woodcut) for Spring Issue, Northwest Review, University of Oregon.

Ferdinand Roten Galleries, Baltimore print dealers, commission editions of "Circle of Love" and "Emerging Woman."

"Circle of Love" (color woodcut) selected for reproduction Book 5, Prize Winning Graphics, Allied Publications, Ft. Lauderdale, Florida.

Sells two paintings to Lee Nordness, Nordness Gallery, New York.

A University Collects: Oregon Pacific Northwest Heritage. Selections from the Haseltine Collection, University of Oregon Museum, circulated by American Federation of Arts.

Northwest Printmakers International, Henry Gallery, University of Washington.

1968   Wins competition to do one of two murals for Portland Civic Auditorium.

One-man Show, Salishan Lodge Gallery, Gleneden, Oregon.

Executes a mural for Ridgewood School, Beaverton, Oregon on animal camouflage.

Begins an association with John Wilson and Lakeside Studios, Michigan. They will sell many prints to college, museum, university collections and arrange a large number of shows of his prints and drawings. John was a top traveling representative for Roten Galleries, Baltimore, handling their shows across the country. He has now formed his own print-making center, offering facilities for visiting printmakers.

One-man Show of Drawings, University of Missouri, Columbia, arranged by Lakeside.

Sells a large selection of prints to Ruth Green, Little Gallery, Raleigh, North Carolina, and the de Cinque Gallery, Miramar, Florida.

1969   Pacific Northwest Art Annual, Erb Memorial Union, University of Oregon.

One-man Show of Prints, Little Gallery, Raleigh, North Carolina.

One-man Show of Drawings and Prints, Washburne University, Topeka.

One-man Show of Paintings, Mt. Hood Community College, Gresham, Oregon.

Receives payment for Civic Auditorium mural but it is not yet installed.

Artists of Oregon 1969, Portland Art Museum.

1970   Drawing Society National Exhibition 1970, circulated by American Federation of Arts: Addison Gallery, Philadelphia Museum, Cooper-Hewitt Museum, the High Museum of Atlanta, Indianapolis Museum, the Museum of Fine Arts in Houston, University of California Gallery in Santa Barbara, Walker Art Center, Portland Art Museum.

Receives Award of Merit, Artists of Oregon Drawings, Watercolors & Collage 1970, Portland Art Museum.

Eleven Oregon Artists, an invitational at Reed College, Portland.

"Out of the Beautiful Past" (woodcut-embossment) purchased by Kalamazoo Art Institute.

Attends special workshop in Japanese printmaking techniques with Junichiro Sekino, Oregon State University, Corvallis.

One-man Show of Drawings, Image Gallery.

Contributes two prints to Spectrum '70, a benefit for building fund, Portland Art Association.

"Man's Past & the Garden of Human Possibilities" finally installed in Civic Auditorium.

1971   Artists of Oregon 1971, Portland Art Museum.

"Flights of Darkness" (acrylic) purchased for collection of Mt. Hood Community College.

One-man Show, Linfield College, McMinnville, Oregon.

Sells a number of woodcuts to editions de la Tortue, Paris.

Makes summer trip to Guadalajara, Mexico City with Barbara.

1972   Works on Paper by Oregon Artists, Portland Art Museum.

"Auto-Show," a one-man Show, Image Gallery.

Statewide Services, University of Oregon, will circulate drawings & prints during 1972-73 to: Erb Memorial Union, University of Oregon; The Dalles Art Club; Mt. Hood Community College; Linn-Benton Community College (Albany); Umpqua Community College (Roseburg); Rogue Valley Art Association (Medford).

"To His Coy Mistress" published by Image Gallery with 4 original woodcuts.

Ferdinand Roten Galleries continues to buy print editions.

Tahir Gallery, New Orleans is now handling prints.

Sells two editions of prints to the Eye Corporation, Chicago.

Takes sabbatical leave from Museum Art School. He will work much of the year under sponsorship of Art Advocates and some 23 individual sponsors.

Spends considerable time with Mary Randlett and Sue Olsen who are developing a photo archive on Northwest artists, planning a documentary book. Randlett has a big, important reputation in Seattle area for her fine photographs of artists including Morris Graves. The book does not materialize; however, Randlett opens files in the art archives, National Portrait Gallery, Smithsonian Institution, on all the artists she has documented.

1973 One-man Show of prints covering 1943-1973, Image Gallery.

Takes the whole family to San Miguel de Allende for the summer, renting a house next door to Collette and Dudley Pratt. The house is beautiful and so is San Miguel.

One-man Show of all work produced for Art Advocates, Image Gallery. It has been a very productive year!

1974 Art of the Pacific Northwest: from the 1930s to the present, National Collection of Fine Arts, Smithsonian Institution. Shown in Washington, D.C., at Seattle Art Museum and Portland Art Museum. His works: "Water Sports" (oil) "Over the Edge" (oil), "World Jumper" (oil) and "Auto-Portrait" (acrylic).

"Japanese Red" (color woodcut) pulled in limited edition of 60 by Neil Borch Jensen, Lakeside Studios. It will be reproduced in the first catalogue of Lakeside Editions. Half the edition goes to Lakeside; half to the Artist. Block is effaced.

1975 Artists of Oregon 1975, Portland Art Museum.

One-man Show, Image Gallery.

A Gift of Love, selections from the Haseltine Collection, University of Oregon Museum.

The Process of Woodcut and Woodengraving, a study exhibit for local circulation, Portland Art Museum.

One-man Show of Paintings and Prints, Hillsboro Public Library.

1976 10th Anniversary Exhibition for Art Advocates. Portland Art Museum. "Some of Us" (acrylic) is reproduced on museum poster for show.

Art for People with More Taste than Money, 34 prints by Northwest printmakers sponsored by Oregon Arts Commission and featured on a poster. "Red Passages" (linocut) is included.

Gives three prints and one painting to the collection of Portland Community College.

1977 "Tracking" (acrylic) purchased for the Oregon Artists Collection, State Capitol, Salem.

Image Gallery publishes "Wind and Pines," Translations from the Ancient Japanese. William Elliott and Noah Brannen are co-translators. Clyde Van Cleve is designer. McLarty creates 8 woodcut-embossments for this limited edition, handbound book. Book is chosen for American Institute of Graphic Arts Book Show 1977, New York, in category of Limited Edition and Fine Private Press Books. It is added to the Rare Book and Manuscript Library of Columbia University by AIGA.

One-man Show of Prints, Keller Gallery, Salem, Oregon.

1978 "Printmaker," an award-winning documentary film by George Johanson and Manson Kennedy documents seven artists including McLarty.

Wins competition for Poster design for the new Portland Mall.

Artquake Invitational Show for 1978, Portland.

Attends intensive 2 week workshop with Akira Kurosaki, Kala Institute, Berkeley.

Visits Japan for the first time. Trip is sponsored by Portland Art Museum and led by Edward Malin. It is a wonderful experience for the small group that goes.

"Wind and Pines" purchased (six copies) by International Communications Agency. Washington, D.C. for prestige showing of American book graphics at international fairs in New Delhi, Belgrade, Leipzig.

Ferdinand Roten Galleries, Baltimore, is bought by Brentano's, marking the end of a distinguished print dealer/publisher. They will commission no more prints by contemporary American printmakers.

1979 Is invited as Guest Printmaker and Instructor in Woodengraving, University of Oregon Art Department Spring Term.

Washington State Art Commission purchases four large works for public schools:
> "The Pool" (acrylic), Barnes Elementary School, Kelso.
> "The Garden" (acrylic), Lakeridge Junior High School, Sumner.
> "Red Bus Man" (acrylic), Blaine High School.
> "Floating World" (acrylic), Helen Haller Elementary School, Sequim.

"Ottos on the Green" (acrylic) purchased by Oregon Arts Commission for the State Transportation Building, Salem.

One-man Show of Paintings, Prints. Pacific University, Forest Grove, Oregon.

"Wind and Pines" most favorably discussed by Sumner Stone, reviewing calligraphic books for Fine Print, A Review for the Arts of the Book, San Francisco.

"Red Passages" (linocut) purchased by Oregon Arts Commission for Southern Oregon College, Ashland.

1980   One-man Show, Image Gallery.

Gives two collographs and three woodcuts to the collection, Southwestern Oregon Community College, Coos Bay.

1981   Takes early retirement from the Museum Art School (Now PNCA), Portland.

1982   Mother dies at age 102.

Executes a design for a stained glass window in a beautiful chapel designed by Walter Gordon for Sacred Heart Church, Newport, Oregon.

One-man Show, Image Gallery.

"Painter as Poet." Jane Van Cleve writes a full-length piece on McLarty for Stepping Out Northwest Summer Issue.

Northwest Prints '82, inaugural exhibition of Northwest Print Council. Portland Art Museum. "Some Dogs in the Fountain" (woodcut), his entry, is later purchased for the Gilkey Collection at the Museum.

Participates in Art Advocates Project for 3 printmakers: Art Hansen, Lyle Matoush and himself. His contribution, "Descent of Man" (color woodcut).

He and Barbara take the trailer to Central Mexico. They are away from November through March 1983. Printmaking with Ralph Gray at Estudio Patzcuaro in Michoacan offers a fine and productive year. They do lots of folkart buying for Image Gallery.

Guest Instructor, teaching a Workshop in Woodcut Techniques with Akira Kurosaki Pacific Northwest College of Art.

1983   Artquake Invitational Show, Portland.

1984   He and Barbara make a fast buying trip to get Eskimo sculpture for a show at Image Gallery. They go to Ottawa and Montreal and, enroute home, stop in New York to visit galleries, museums. She is thrilled to meet Joe and Ruth Solman at last.

Sapporo-Portland Print Show, an exchange exhibition, Portland State University.

1985   One-man Show, an invitational in the Governor's Office. State Capitol, Salem.

Waterworks, a one-man Show, Wentz Gallery, Pacific Northwest College of Art.

"Butterfly Dogs" (color woodcut) purchased for Salem Public Library, Salem, Oregon.

Northwest Print Council Exhibition, North Central Washington Museum, Wenatchee.

Contributes a print to Portfolio for Alumni and Friends, Pacific Northwest College of Art.

Four Printmakers Show, Rogue Gallery, Medford, Oregon.

Retrospective Show of Prints & Selected Paintings, Pacific University, Forest Grove, Oregon.

Western States Print Invitational, Portland Art Museum.

Commemorates 24th year of Image Gallery with an original color woodcut and poster.

Illustrates "Going in with the Guerrillas," by Robert Ellis Gordon, Clinton Street Quarterly Summer Issue.

Conducts Printmaking Workshop with Elaine Chandler/Dennis Cunningham/Pacific Northwest College of Art, New Horizons in Printmaking.

1986   The McLartys leave Northwest Portland after a residence of 40 years. He joins a congenial group of artists in Troy Studios on the Eastside. They sell the Image Gallery to Beverly Shoemaker.

Image Gallery publishes "Encounters with the White Train," by Andy Robinson. It contains McLarty woodcuts as illustrations.

Retrospective Show of Paintings and Prints, Maude Kerns Art Center, Eugene.

1987   Five person Print Show, Image Gallery that includes: Bill Colby, William Givler, Art Hansen, McLarty and Mery Lynn McCorkle.

1988   Forty Oregon Printmakers with catalogue sponsored by Oregon Arts Commission and Northwest Print Council. "The Devil Lives Under Ocumicho" (linocut) reproduced.

Designs the first of three posters he will do for "Designed to Wear," an annual show of original, wearable art, a benefit for Oregon School of Arts and Crafts, Portland.

One-man Show, Jack McLarty: Paintings from the Past Five Years, Wentz Gallery, Portland Art Museum. Monograph by John S. Weber, Adjunct Curator, Oregon Art Institute.

One-man Show, Image Gallery.

Is included in Artists' Liaison Exhibition Catalogue, Venice, California.

1989   Is invited to show in Six Pacific Northwest Artists: More Blue is Bluer. Organized by Gwen Stone, Shasta College, Redding, California.

"Hopalong" (oil) from the Haseltine Collection, University of Oregon Museum, is reproduced on back cover, Smart Art published by Zephyr Press, Tucson. It is a textbook for art instructors.

Is reproduced in California Art Review, Chicago, Illinois.

Leaving in February, spends several months on a trailer trip with Barbara to Central Mexico.

1990   "Flower Vendor" (color woodcut) reproduced in Art of Print-making published by Northwest Print Council, Portland.

Juries Sixth Annual Human Form Exhibition, Oregon Coast Council for the Arts, Newport.

Executes a mural, "Mind Space," for Buckman School under the One Percent for Arts Program, Portland Public Schools.

Designs his second poster for "Designed to Wear," a benefit for Oregon School of Arts and Crafts.

Produces the "Book of Color," sponsored by Art Advocates. It contains 8 color woodcuts; is handbound. Nancy N. Ramsey is designer. The edition is 60.

1991   After 5 years of condo-apartment living, the McLartys opt for an older house at 3123 N.E. Broadway. It offers studio space on third floor, considerable storage, is zoned for business and they like the location mid-way between Lloyd Center and Hollywood. Much work needs to be done but it is a wonderful house!

One-man Show of Prints from 1974-1990, Image Gallery.

Executes a design for stained glass windows at Laurelhurst School under the One Percent for Arts Program. Hal Bond does production and installation.

Designs a third poster for "Designed to Wear," Oregon School of Arts & Crafts.

After a year or so of being restricted by angina, he is advised to do so and he undergoes by-pass surgery. All activities are suspended for a good many weeks. His recovery goes very well.

1992   Works on a series of woodcuts which he can cut and hand-color with minimal stress, and a number of small, intense pastels of flowers and garden-rooms.

Nell Givler has started him on orchid growing.

"The Devil Lives Under Ocumicho" is used for cover and illustrations, "Extinction," Spring Issue 1992 Left Bank #2, Blue Heron Publishing, Hillsboro, Oregon.

1993   West Coast Edition Printmakers, an invitational, Claudia Chapline Gallery, Stinson Beach, California.

50 year Retrospective, the collection of Mayo Rolph Roy, Linfield College, McMinnville, Oregon. Discusses his work with slide-lecture.

Contributes to Art Futures, a benefit for Pacific Northwest College of Art.

L.A. Society of Printmakers, Woodland Hills, California.

Participates in 101 Prints, a benefit for Friends of the Gilkey Center, Portland Art Museum and Northwest Print Council.

One-man Show, McLartys' Choice Gallery, Portland.

"Powell's Books" (woodcut) purchased for the Visual Chronicle of Portland.

Gives a copy of "Wind and Pines" and one woodcut to the University of New Mexico Museum.

Is invited to serve on Advisory Committee for Visual Chronicle of Portland.

1994   "The Sugar Angel" (color woodcut) commissioned by Northwest Print. Council as one of several gift prints available to Associate Members.

Contributes to Art Futures, a benefit for Pacific Northwest College of Art.

Jack McLarty: Portland Paintings of the Forties and Fifties, McLartys' Choice Gallery.

Invitational Print Show, University of Hawaii, Hilo.

One-man Show of Prints, Graven Images Gallery, Ashland, Oregon.

Gives "Dental Clinic" (acrylic) to Dental School, Oregon Health Sciences University, Portland.

20. *The Fountain of Youth* (oil) 1959 43 x 66

Two widely held notions about fine arts are false, and Lillie Lauha is just the person to prove it. The first notion she attacks head on…" Those who say that Oregon is a backwater, that there's nothing going on here, are wrong. We have an Oregon school of art, separate, that stands on its own…She has been closely following the careers of the artists who make up that Oregon school, collecting their major works and working to expand public access to the arts for 30 years. In so doing she has disproven the second major myth: that collecting fine art – major works by painters and sculptors of note – is the exclusive pursuit of the very wealthy. Employed for many years as Office Manager for a Portland coffee importing firm, Miss Lauha began in 1950 to buy paintings and sculpture, prints and ceramics, a piece at a time from then largely unrecognized artists…often stretching out payments over a period of time. "I didn't do it for financial reasons," she said. "I bought things that I could respond to, that affected me." Canvases she bought for $150 to $300 might be worth 10 times that amount today. Her comfortable apartment in a Southwest Portland high-rise has its walls covered with canvases large and small by artists whose names are highlights in the Oregon catalog: Louis Bunce, Jack McLarty, Manuel Izquierdo, Lee Kelly, etc. Tastes and reactions to art are changing, she said, and what was controversial at one time is several years later part of the landscape. Witness the subsiding controversies over sculpture on the Portland Mall and the Louis Bunce at the Portland International Airport. One explanation for that, Miss Lauha said, is that *a good artist is an especially good observer of the world.* Some things that they see first…we see more readily after a little more time, especially after they have shown us the way. An example of such "vision" can be found in one of Jack McLarty's canvases in the Lauha Collection…McLarty is a visual punster of a painter…he uses identifiable images, but what they might represent is another matter. In *Fountain of Youth* human figures of various scales cavort in pools and ledges of a multi-tiered outdoor fountain. Some are partially clad revelers nearly drowning in their sensuality; others, apparently a part of a verbal play on the title. A large nude made of melting ice-cream like material is being attacked by a giant spoon while nearby a banana-split boat carries more revelers across the top of a dome that resembles nothing so much as a huge jello mold. The whole effect of moving water, sunlit sensuality and sprawling humanity evokes Ira's Fountain by the Civic Auditorium. But the painting predates construction of the fountain by several years….

Alan Hayakawa, *The Oregonian,* June 22, 1980.

21. *In the Air* (oil) 1959 66 x 44

This department has often complained about the fact that our lines of artistic communication stretch almost exclusively eastward, with the result that we know next to nothing about artistic goings-on in Los Angeles and have learned about the Pacific Northwest School mainly because it is highly regarded in New York. The Ruthermore Galleries, however, are doing something about this deplorable situation with a show of paintings and sculpture by artists of Portland …The show seems to be an outgrowth of the Oregon Centennial Exhibition…which opens next week in Portland…trade fairs of the past were major outlets for American artists, but in recent years the painters and sculptors have largely been omitted…I suspect that Portland has had few such art shows since its Lewis and Clark Exposition in 1905…

The Ruthermore show is one of those group events so full of differing personalities that one can write about it only in the most general terms. Abstract Expressionism dominates…(but) the show also goes most successfully to the opposite extreme…(among three examples mentioned) the vivid dynamism of Jack McLarty's painting….

Alfred Frankenstein, *San Francisco Chronicle,* June 5, 1959.

About 2 years ago it was my privilege to judge an art show organized by the Oregon Art Alliance in the galleries of the University of Oregon (Museum) in Eugene. There were many good things in that show *but the one that took first prize beyond all doubt* (emphasis added) was a large dramatic 'Crucifixion' painted by Jack McLarty of Portland. Now this same Jack McLarty has a show at the Ruthermore Gallery in San Francisco and it also contains a 'crucifixion' but one of a very different sort…This picture is actually called *Forest Figure* and it may well be a comment on what man does to the forest, although aesthetic considerations, especially light-soaked color and vivid, brilliant brushwork, play the primary role in McLarty's work. It is full of symbolism….He packs an outrageous satire worthy of Breughel if not of Bosch into such paintings as *Fountain of Youth* …because of soft, fuzzy outlines and indistinct focus, the figures of this satire take a long time in making themselves known…For a quick look I recommend things like *In the Air* with its big, ascending, spraying and flying forms….

Alfred Frankenstein, *San Francisco Chronicle,* August 27, 1961.

22. *Voyage of the Neon Horse* (oil) 1958 43 x 68

23. *Autumn Storm* (*Leaf Storm*) (oil) c 1960 40 x 48

24. *Fallen Lovers* (oil) 1960 67 x 42

25. *Rain Figure* (oil) 1961 50 x 50

26. *Blue Bouquet* (oil) 1961 36 x 32

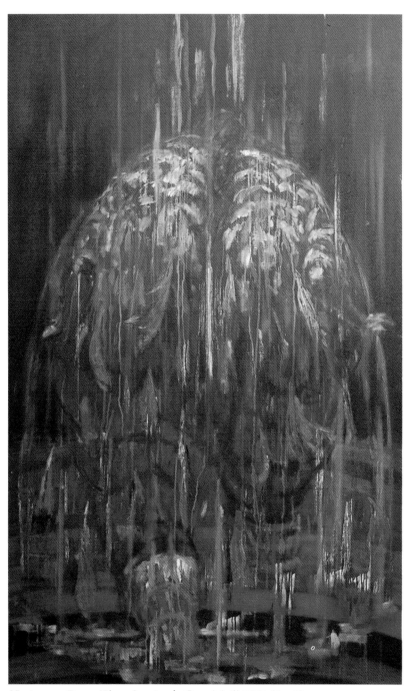

27. *Autumn Figure (Player Leaving the Game)* (oil) 1961 66 x 42

28. *Run Past the Stands* (oil) 1960 48 x 37

Few persons observe sports more keenly than does Jack McLarty, the oft-honored Portland artist whose 18th one-man exhibition since 1945 opens Sunday at Image Gallery...Most of the paintings in the show are the outgrowth of such observation. But McLarty's paintings are not literal. He uses sports as other things that human beings do, to add vividness to ideas he wishes to convey. He paints not only in a highly individualistic style but often the canvas and paint are the media for biting satire and sparkling humor. His paintings are revealing about the inner man because (he) transfers his thinking to canvas as a poet or writer does with the written word.

His latest paintings in this show stem from the time when he was concentrating particularly on running figures of football players ...from the running figures he changed to jumping ones, and the field became more of a curved edge of a stage that finally evolved into the edge of the world...

In some of these the casual observer might find it difficult to associate the round form tumbling in space as an athlete, although it may wear the colors or uniform of, say, a hockey player. In the metaphorical transition such figures might seem more like balloons floating in space while others rolling along the field might make one think of gaily colored Easter eggs....

Louise Aaron, *Portland Reporter,* April 27, 1962.

29. *Giant Runner* (oil) 1962-63 65 x 43

30. *The Hat Game* (oil) 1962 19 x 47

The retrospective exhibition of the work of Jack McLarty which will open to the public at the Portland Art Museum at noon Wednesday, reveals a painter preoccupied with the psychological climate of contemporary times and the inner lives of those existing in that climate.

What McLarty has to say is said with a masterly brush, limitless imagination and an originality seldom seen in contemporary paintings. His statements are those of a keen and often witty...observer....

Here is an artist who is willing to say, "This is what is happening to me, to my family, my friends, to all. This is the world in which we live – beautiful, ugly beyond belief, trivial, great, superficial, full of terrifying depths, gay, dark with the agony of loneliness – a world of sharp contrasts and never fully definable nor understandable.

The retrospective is not one to be viewed on a half hour lunch period. It will require many visits for full comprehension and enjoyment, for McLarty is a master of the metaphorical idiom and translation of his meanings, subtly recorded in infinite variety on his canvasses, is not done with ease and speed. Only as the viewer relates his own inner self and emotions, as they react to the contemporary scene, will he begin to read and possibly understand canvas content in this exhibition reviewing one artist's 20 years of observing man and his world. The artist's great versatility, imagination and originality is seen in his employment of many symbols, ever changing but always identifiable. The child, one such recurring figure, may be...isolated (or) sharply defined (as) in *Conflagration Point*, as it extends an inquisitive hand toward upward curving flames that threaten to engulf the unconcerned world about him....The child...becomes the symbol of man unaware of the world that he has entered, oblivious alike to the joys and disasters that he will find there. There is wit, both keen and subtle, in *The Anatomy Lesson*, where a small boy huddles under an arch intent on his book while on the beach before him cavort the luscious figures of the bikini clad.

Catherine Jones, *The Oregonian*, September 22, 1963.

31. *World Jumper #2* (oil) 1962 66 x 42

32. *Little Song* (oil) 1960 45 x 34

33. *The Anatomy Lesson* (oil) 1963 50 x 57

34. *Over the Edge* (oil) 1963 42 x 66

35. *Le Mabillon* (oil) 1964 42 x 66

We don't know why Jack McLarty's paintings remind us of Paul Klee, unless it's because of their seemingly inexhaustible elusive content with a richness that viewers can browse through, with surprises lurking here and there – and with the surprises continuing to re-form... in the viewing process....Only one painting (in the current show) originated in a direct way from his recent sabbatical tour for travel and study in Europe. *Cafe Mabillon*...The incredibly complex cast in the painting, which looks like a population explosion, was observed during the cafe sitting he says he finally became accustomed to doing. At Le Mabillon, McLarty said he noted that artists, students and others just met, talked, wrote letters, etc. It recalled things he had done years before as a student. "I rushed around the last three evenings sketching..." And it is from the sketches that he has marshaled a complex, animated, crowded order on the canvas...In a way he says that he supposes that his canvases which are brimming with complex compositions are a substitute for doing murals which were part of his early interest.

Since what he is interested in doing content-wise is not the kind of content that seems to fit within the more decorative work usually sought for buildings – though there have been periods in art when it would have been –like a good many artists who would like doing murals, he feels that what he could do in them would (probably) be less important to him than what he can do on a canvas. "As an artist I'm involved in the social scene in its different aspects all the way through. Perhaps it's a little like Stuart Davis putting order into disorder; and *if you're going to deal with social content a great deal of the time, then part of your function is to correct imbalances in society* (emphasis added). It's a participation in the social scene, not just standing aside or making a positive statement. You don't really control that society, you just live within it..." And in dealing with social content, (he) says, "You touch on sensitive areas..." McLarty brings so much to his work, including occasional lightning touches of wit..."

Beth Fagan, *The Oregonian,* April 1965.

36. *In the Green Region* (oil) 1964 36 x 36

I am sure you don't remember us, as I doubt if we've met, but I first noticed your work at a Reed Arts Festival. Those festivals were a great success, particularly at the beginning...I well remember the last one, in the Spring of '60, and I'm sure you were there...We were there as ex-Reedites, my husband having retired from teaching literature...and I had left the faculty earlier, to do piano teaching at home. We moved to Seattle where my husband had a job at the University of Washington...we had both taught there before going to Reed....One of the docents asked me how I liked it (the Invitational Painting Show for Oregon, Washington and British Columbia organized by Portland Art Museum for the centennial year 1959). I told her Washington was poorly represented – all of Oregon work was excellent and the B.C. work mostly unknown but interesting. I said to the docent, "Come with me and I'll show you the best pictures in the show." I led her to your lovely pictures. "There, these are all marvelous, my favorites in the show." And she heartily agreed with me....

personal letter from **Edna W. Chittick** *to the Artist, March 4, 1964.*

Some of my friends have been looking at my lovely little *Nude* (Blue Nude) with a dubious eye and some, I suspect, with outright disapproval...and did I tell Jack he had even been attacked in print, from a surprisingly liberal source, as pornographic? Seems to me it was *my picture* (emphasis added) that was under attack as I do not remember any other nude and, if is pornographic, then I haven't grown up, as I am utterly unable to see it that way. One gentleman did comment that she looked "accessible" which, after all, is his business and not mine! So it goes in the wonderful world of art. If everyone were approving, you might begin to feel yourself a failure....

personal letter from **Edna W. Chittick** *to* **Barbara McLarty,** *July 20, 1964.*

37. *The Lost Colour* (oil) 1965 50 x 50

38. *Cloak of Memory* (oil) 1965 66 x 44

39. *Tracking* (oil) 1966-67 46½ x 66½

40. *Icarus in Green* (oil) 1966 18 x 14

Jack McLarty is a painter whose work stems from surrealism. He creates complex statements of great mental and pictorial agility that reach far beyond mere visual punning and incredible juxtaposition. His work covers the vast range of emotion and feeling from tender, lyrical intimacy to the frightening threats which trouble man's existence, from Rabelaisian laughter to grief, from playful, exuberant games to the shock of sometimes insoluble discrepancies of life.... McLarty gives us no ordinary, everyday reality but a poetic one... A nude upon a bed is also a beautiful landscape...

The voluminous jumpers of earlier canvases, so hopelessly weighted down and caught within a pictorial frame, now turn and face the viewer with (sometimes) ominous...indefinable burdens and nameless, extravagant gear...When we look at *The Junk Man*, we are seeing ourselves, we are seeing the Artist, we are seeing Everyman.

McLarty's paint surface is always tightly controlled. There is nothing haphazard about the many layers of paint and the washes of color he applies. He insists that the medium support his ideas instead of allowing fortuitous occurrences in the act of painting to dictate results that may give us a "happening" on canvas.

Madeleine R. Liepe, March 1, 1967.

41. *Empty Runner* (oil) 1967 66 x 44

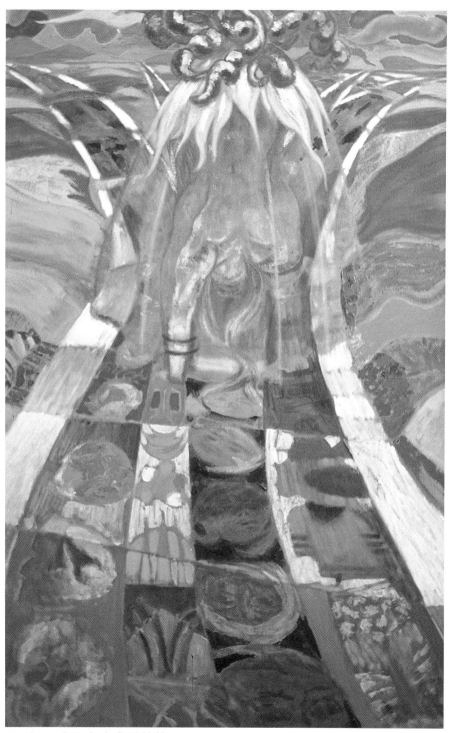

42. *The Road Divides* (oil) 1966 68 x 44

43. *The Burden* (oil) 1967 48 x 48

At the Image Gallery Jack McLarty offers his observations in a very personal stream-of-consciousness format. (His) paintings...focus sharply on the individual and surround him with his myriad problems, puzzlements and, sometimes, occasional intensely felt delights.... *The Junk Man* and *The Burden* painted in that order, both use the pneumatic, blown-up figures familiar in previous works. But in the newer canvases the figure is not so much buoyed up by the inflation as surrounded and almost suffocated by it. These two paintings, as complete statement, first have the effect of giving a hardy wallop and then, as detail is studied (and McLarty paints in great detail), a chuckle replaces the shock of the painting's visual impact. The viewer has discovered that the vast pile of psychological and sociological junk that the almost obscured *Junk Man* is attempting to carry, acquires in *The Burden* a transparency that makes the burdens meaningless as problems. The inflated figure plodding on and on, is unaware of the change in weight. He still thinks he has problems, and the viewer reaches the artist's conclusion that "Life is like that."...

McLarty is always subjective, never literal, even when he presents a beautiful and perfect nude as he often does, either as a focus for his theme or as a unit in his extremely delicate canvases....

McLarty says his paintings show life as he sees it, a natural process with patterns of growth as extended by man often becoming extremely complicated – appearing and disappearing in his canvases. Both nature and people, he says, try all kinds of things, some successful, some not – but all are part of the unfolding of the life of the individual. We live in a very complex world but it has patterns and rhythms....

Catherine Jones, *The Oregonian*, March 3, 1967.

44. *The Junk Man* (oil) 1965 48 x 48

45. *Children in the Air* (oil) 1966 (a detail is shown) 36 x 30

46. *Patterns of Love* (oil) c. 1968 36 x 36

47. *The Red Room* (acrylic) 1969 66 x 44

48. *Utamaro's House* (acrylic) 1969 48 x 48

49. *The Other Room* (acrylic) 1969 48 x 48

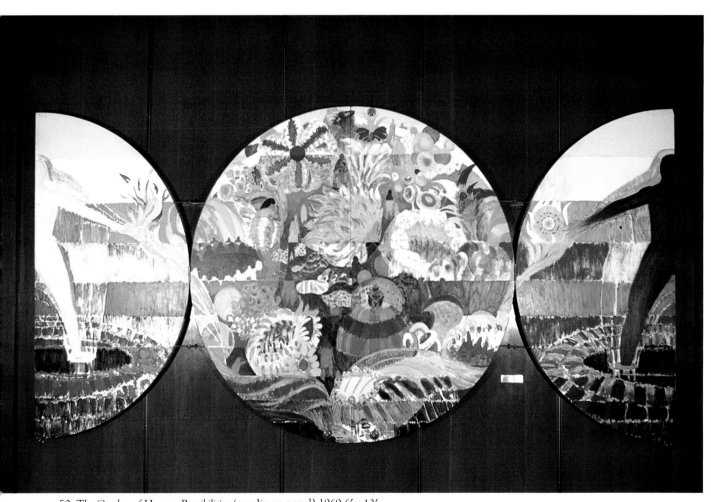

50. *The Garden of Human Possibilities* (acrylic on panel) 1969 6' x 12'

51. *Flights of Darkness* (acrylic) 1971 44 x 66

52. *The Passing Scene* (acrylic) 1971 36 x 36

53. *A Big Red One* (acrylic) 1970-71 66 x 44

54. *The Green Room* (acrylic) 1973 48 x 48

55. *Japanese Red* (acrylic) 1973 24 x 24

56. *The Heart of John Donne (The Legacy)* (acrylic) 1972-73 36 x 37½

57. *Black and White Post* (acrylic on wood) 71 x 10 x 10

58. *Light in a Room* (pastel) 1973 40 x 30

59. *A Walk Through the Woods* (acrylic) 1974 29 x 41

60. *The Great Flood of 1974* (acrylic) 1974 39½ x 49

61. *General Motors* (Auto-Portrait) (acrylic) 1972 43 x 65

In comparing the art of Jack McLarty to the work of other artists that I know, I find his work is unique because almost everything he creates is a comment on the world around us. While others depict flowers and clouds and landscapes and, as far as I am concerned, turn their backs to the world we live in, producing nothing that reflects our time except, perhaps, the fear of being considered controversial and the fear of being barred from the marketplace, his work relates to us as human beings. We can respond not only intellectually but also emotionally – with sorrow, joy, laughter and anger and, too, a feeling of serenity because of a moment of beauty.

In McLarty, from the earliest work and continuing today, we find a commentator on the world around us – the butcher shops in the Farmers' Market with their hanging carcasses so like humans, impaled on the hooks of a merciless society – the people of the skidroad, onlookers of a world that has passed them by – the gentle sarcasm (and sometimes not so gentle) in his paintings concerning our "festivals"…his football players – his bulky earthbound figures lumbering into space – our love affair with the automobile – and the desecration of our cities…

Nick Chaivoe, August 1975.

74

62. *Warm Room (Dark Room)* (acrylic) c. 1975 48 x 48

63. *The Ballad of Arn-Nicklaus* (acrylic) 1975 42 x 66

Living with Jack McLarty's paintings is an exhilarating experience. My first picture dates back to the jazzman period (the forties). This small, blue picture has been a companion through all sorts of living conditions. It has taken on depth, meaning and beauty...In living with this small piece, the viewer becomes involved in adding to the meaning of the Artist...and in so doing, one has a record of the time, and also the passing of time....As soon as one limits Jack to a "message" I think one overlooks the organic unity of his paintings which forever make the demand that the viewer broaden his own experience...Another painting (I own) is the *Ballad of Arn-Nicklaus*. The subject matter is common – no question that the common sights are there. Even non-golfers have the experience of golf as an American activity and internationally we are aware of it...(it) opens up a whole new vista for those who golf as well as those who do not. The feeling of the land, the tools of the game, the people of all varieties who are on the course – the feelings and the emotions of those playing and those watching – all are incorporated...the human dimensions of a popular cult take on artistic meaning....Jack has shown the temporality yet universality of human activities in groups; he invites social comment yet he has opened the door to individual reflection....One must take the time and risk the jolt that he may see something new that doesn't fit preconceived notions...it is an opportunity to perceive, feel and think beyond our present, immediate activity.

Mayo Rae Rolph Roy, August 1975.

64. *Bus to "XoXo"* (acrylic) 1975 26 x 52

65. *Just Take the First Road* (acrylic) 1975 39 x 39

66. *Activity Along the Willamette* (acrylic) 1975 30 x 62

Some of my friends have been looking at my lovely little *Nude* (Blue Nude) with a dubious eye and some, I suspect, with outright disapproval…and did I tell Jack he had even been attacked in print, from a surprisingly liberal source, as pornographic? Seems to me it was *my picture* (emphasis added) that was under attack as I do not remember any other nude and, if is pornographic, then I haven't grown up, as I am utterly unable to see it that way. One gentleman did comment that she looked "accessible" which, after all, is his business and not mine! So it goes in the wonderful world of art. If everyone were approving, you might begin to feel yourself a failure….

personal letter from **Edna W. Chittick** *to* **Barbara McLarty,** *July 20, 1964.*

I am sure you don't remember us, as I doubt if we've met, but I first noticed your work at a Reed Arts Festival. Those festivals were a great success, particularly at the beginning…I well remember the last one, in the Spring of '60, and I'm sure you were there…We were there as ex-Reedites, my husband having retired from teaching literature…and I had left the faculty earlier, to do piano teaching at home. We moved to Seattle where my husband had a job at the University of Washington…we had both taught there before going to Reed….One of the docents asked me how I liked it (the Invitational Painting Show for Oregon, Washington and British Columbia organized by Portland Art Museum for the centennial year 1959). I told her Washington was poorly represented – all of Oregon work was excellent and the B.C. work mostly unknown but interesting. I said to the docent, "Come with me and I'll show you the best pictures in the show." I led her to your lovely pictures. "There, these are all marvelous, my favorites in the show." And she heartily agreed with me….

personal letter from **Edna W. Chittick** *to the Artist, March 4, 1964.*

67. *In Pretty Deep* (acrylic) 1977-78 36 x 36

68. *Chac* (acrylic on panel) c. 1983 72 x 48

69. *Totems* (acrylic on wood) c. 1984

70. *Sculpture for Artquake* (acrylic on wood) 1984 86 x 172

71. *Underground* (acrylic) 1978 40 x 20

72. *River City Life* (acrylic) 1979 40 x 50

At first glance, Jack McLarty's paintings appear to be festive with vivid colors…a child's building blocks of joy. However, at closer inspection the acrylic paintings reveal a chain of ominous images: smoking nuclear reactors, babies strangling fish and drowning dolls, and legions of blinking machines….One of the exhibit's highlights was the awesome acrylic puzzle, *River City Life*. It depicts a chubby, golden baby strangling the life out of a fish as tinker toy planes crash into its skull. Haphazard machine outlines and televisions on the blink form an ironically lush background in viridian and cerulean blue. In my opinion, the painting comments on the stunted growth of a new generation and a new technological society…the violence against nature that our man-made jungle breeds. Another glowing example of McLarty's work is the painting, *The River Heats Up*. The center is comprised of machines of yellow-orange oblong blocks that unfurl like snakes, hovering at river's edge. The river is Portland's Willamette, as the city outline registers with the viewer. Bordering this scene are contemporary hieroglyphics which seem to blink and do somersaults. These primitive symbols remind the viewer of smoking volcanoes, helicopters, tanks and weapons. Also Saturn and Mars appear, ominously throbbing. McLarty comments on society in a playfully deceptive way. It takes some thought to figure out the action and, then, make the underlying connections. Effortlessly, he can balance composition and comment…at times the artist's work can be too cryptic. Or maybe those are the paintings that take a lot more meditation than most of us have the patience for…But watch out! His visual power and (his) emotional impact will linger long after.

Wendla McGovern, *Gallery Review*, September 1982.

73. *Evidence of Passage* (acrylic) 1978 42 x 64

74. *The Garden* (acrylic) 1978 40 x 60

There is much to be said for doing your own thing – and when it comes to some of Oregon's better-known older artists, we see it as a sign of maturity that so many do not feel a need to change their course of direction simply for the sake of being thought up-to-date. Hereabouts, it isn't as if artists were unaware of the new ideas which emanate with incredible frequency from such major centers as Los Angeles and New York. Rather, in this age which features a communications industry that constantly engages in overkill – including much analysis and touting of arts developments which at times are quite half-baked – it comes as amazing that more artists have not been rendered catatonic by the bombardment of dictums as to what they should and should not be doing. At the local level...local galleries this month afford a heartening experience in that they provide evidence that there are people here who seem quite content to develop within those areas for which they so long have worked....Best evidence of this right now occurs at the Fountain Gallery...with George Johanson...in an exhibition that surprises by its diversity and technical virtuosity; and at the Image Gallery, where Jack McLarty...holds forth with brand new paintings and prints that amply indicate that he has not lost his genius for social commentary....McLarty dots his highly patterned, neon-hued canvases and wood engravings with all kinds of creatures – from a muscular river goddess astride a calico cat to toy-like, anthropomorphical versions of automobiles and insects. His humor is gentle but it does boast an edge. He enjoys civic celebrations, organized pageants; he relishes the color, the buffoonery of such celebrations. He is both intrigued and horrified by the garishness and pomposity of so many middle-American rituals, sports and pastimes, from gambling in Las Vegas to beauty contests...McLarty and Johanson share a kindred philosophical outlook. Both offer statements that will strike some viewers as unduly cynical... But both artists try to truly reflect the emotional atmosphere of the times in which we now live.

Andy Rocchia, *Journal Art Editor,* April 17, 1980.

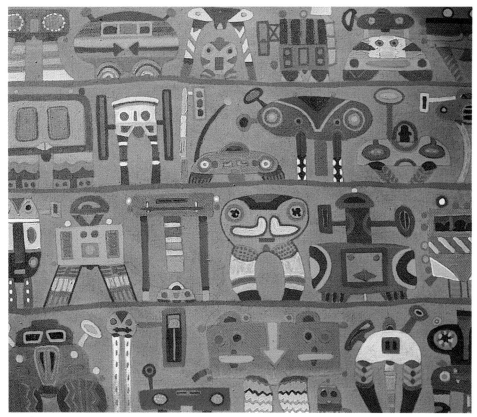

75. *Ottos on the Green* (acrylic) 1979 38 x 48

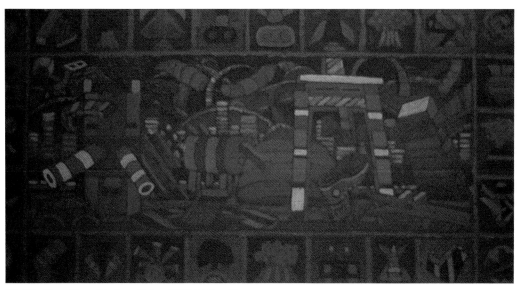

76. *The River Heats Up* (acrylic) c. 1980 21¼ x 41

77. *The Inside/Outside Room* (acrylic) c. 1979 52 x 40

87

78. *The Prophet* (acrylic) 1982 48 x 36

79. *The Dirty Babies* (acrylic) 1981 36 x 36

Things are not good in Jack McLarty's dark-green and purple world. In his urgent, dense acrylic paintings (1980-82) absolutely every surface has been filled with a color or a pattern or an image that speaks of the ill-turnings of the world. Many of the paintings depict a seamy Portland, and the Willamette River is central to several of them. In a merciless portrayal of the city, *The Dirty Babies* (the title is wonderful), big, round and green, black-edged babies are half-sitting in a cluttered river. They play with some kind of airborne contraptions that have been painted with zig-zagged day-glo pinks and purples. Juxtaposed against the babies, these bright shapes take on great power, the colors fairly lunging at you, and one notices immediately how this day-glo pattern repeats itself throughout the painting. These zig-zags are in many of McLarty's works, and are eloquent expressionist gestures. Beyond the babies and the water and the boats, and nestled among a hill of television sets (all filled with bright stripes of color), hover forbiddingly round, green-black men. What distinguishes them from each other are their neckties and the shape of their heads.One has only a hat for a head, another, a rectangle....

Sabrina Ullman, *Willamette Week,* November 1982.

80. *Giant in Trouble* (acrylic) 1982 48 x 37

81. *Willamette Wars* (acrylic) 1982 40 x 50

82. *Hungry Baby* (acrylic) 1986 36 x 36

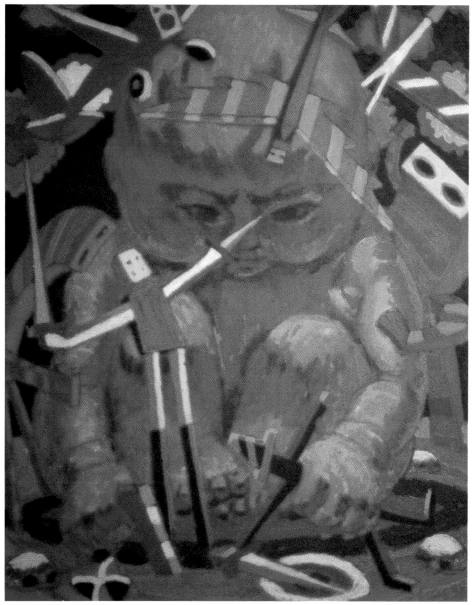

83. *Red Baby* (acrylic) 1987 49 x 37

84. *The East Side as the Garden of Eden* (acrylic) 1985 43 x 73

There is a recurring figure among the dark acrylic paintings Jack McLarty is showing at the Image Gallery. A demonic baby Buddha, huge and naked, wilfully destructive dominates some of the canvases and is tucked away in others. The baby is a bad dream. He scowls or laughs madly and tears at the toys around him. Blocks tumble; airplanes are plucked out of middair and crushed; a baby perched on the banks of the Willamette reaches into the water to grab a fish. He squeezes a long red tongue out of it.

As the jumbo toddler creates chaos around him, long robot arms snake around him. The robot toy soldiers are grim and threatening but the baby plays on, oblivious to their presence, fulfilling the moment by destroying whatever is close. McLarty is a satirist...and symbols come easily to these canvases. The giant child might represent any number of things: the self-absorption of the human, making him blind to the threats of the technological; the threat of the younger generation to the older; the stupidity of hedonism; the fearfulness the modern condition ought to inspire in us. Whatever it is that McLarty is getting at, it is awfully bleak!....*The East Side as*

the Garden of Eden seems innocent enough at first glance. There are recognizable landmarks – the US Bancorp Tower, Union Station, a stylized erupting Mt. St Helens, a more realistic Mt. Hood. There are jungle cats with red spots, an apple tree, the Hawthorne Bridge, a naked couple walking westward, a profile of God, and two Indians peeking over the Cascades. But closer inspection reveals a large spider tramping into town, toppled buildings, the back of a bald corpulent naked man bursting out of a coffin. The dim light, the flat surface of the painting, and a sickly yellow out-sized pig with ruby eyes lead the viewer to inescapable conclusions about the world...McLarty has inhabited this turf for a long time...(he) is an original. The paintings in this show seem unrelated to art movements, fashions or schools. The imagery is personal...(It) is so personal that it may do him a disservice to categorize him. His paintings work at an emotional level...even though their sources seem to be more cerebral – the workings of a very critical mind.

Barry Johnson, *The Oregonian*, October 1, 1986.

85. *Children of the Mind* (acrylic) 1987 60 x 44

86. *Blues* (acrylic) 1986 48 x 36

Jack McLarty has been a vigorous force in the Portland art scene for so long that he tends, unjustly, to be taken for granted. He is a regional artist in the best sense of the term, using his immediate environment, both physical and social, as a vehicle for his observations and his feelings about the quintessential human issues – death, war, dignity, joy. Trenchant social awareness mixed with humor and a dash of whimsy are set forth in surrealistic, richly colored imagery…Although always figurative, many paintings are so dense that their closely woven negative and positive spaces can be seen as abstract patterns…. The dominant theme (in his work) has been and continues to be the inability of humans to recognize much less accept their common plight and common needs. The frenetic activity that we engage in to avoid confronting society's awful problems has been seen in…past work…but in recent years the cloak of revelry has been shed. In McLarty's current show at Image Gallery, as in last year's major exhibition at Pacific Northwest College of Art, he interprets the world of children at play, presenting it as parallel to the world of adults. The obsession with toys – toys that take control of their owners and assume a life of their own – makes for an horrific view of contemporary society. Using a monstrous, malevolent baby as the central image, he fills the canvas with toy cars, airplanes, boats, robots and stick figures, a few of which the baby gleefully clutches and destroys while the others wreak their own mayhem around him….In other work McLarty turns his (subconscious) attention to stick figures engaged in their own play, to a bag lady with wondrous objects stuffed in the many pockets of her coat and an umbrella that shields her from gargantuan rain drops (*The Rain Queen*)….No doubt all of McLarty's work is about his own devils – some playful – others chillingly bleak. One wishes for a major retrospective that would show the evolution and connections in an important and richly varied body of work.

Lois Allan, *Artweek*, October 22, 1988.

87. *The Rain Queen* (acrylic) 1988 60 x 43

88. *Aqua Dreams* (acrylic) 1989 45 x 40

89. *Dreams of a Golf Lover* (acrylic) 1990 44 x 40

90. *World Baby* (acrylic) 1987 60 x 45

I'm here in the gallery enjoying myself sitting surrounded by your paintings…Color surrounds us. Still it comes down to expression. How it dances and lives in your paintings. It's rewarding to sit and absorb ideas and themes and experimentations from your sure knowledge and hand and heart. The problem for me these days is so many shows lack depth. Your show is a real treat for the eyes.

personal letter to the Artist from **Kathleen McCuistion,** *artist and former student, May 31, 1991.*

91. *Lynda the Cat Goddess* (acrylic) 1993 48 x 48

92. *The New Baby* (acrylic) 1994 48 x 48

93. *Mind Space* (acrylic on panel) 1990 7′ x 20′

Buckman Elementary School students have watched day by day as Portland artist Jack McLarty paints a mural for their building. They have asked questions and even posed for some of the work… Students from the city's new elementary arts magnet school will share their feelings and interpretation of the mural through art, dance, drama and writing at a dedication celebration. The mural, named *Mind Space*, covers a 15 foot long wall just inside the entrance to the school. It is a bright, imaginative work that incorporates a galaxy of planets, each with a special theme – a garden planet, a rain planet, a planet filled with books and children reading, and a planet populated by the Portland Trail Blazers. The Buckman mural is the fourth art project to be dedicated in a series of 22 planned collaborations between Portland Public Schools and the 1 percent for Arts Program.

Suzanne Richards, *The Oregonian,* October 7, 1990.

102

I believe that art is like a seed. That it contains, in capsule form, the society in which it is produced. Art takes the temperature of the time of its birth and tells the health or sickness, the anger or peace, the dreams or realities of that particular period and place.

Statement by the Artist, 1990.

Between the river and the rain lies the city. Saturated with dark and light. Life streams that join heaven and earth. Truth flows through the center city and the center body. The pools glitter with reflections of the color and the concerns of the creatures within. What water does to light and what color does to darkness and what people do, is what I like – water isn't everything but in Portland it is more than enough.

Statement by the Artist, 1985.

94. *An Unfinished Life* (acrylic) 1994 54 x 39

Jack McLarty's window for the small Sacred Heart chapel in Newport is, in my opinion, one of the finest contemporary stained glass works in the country. The chapel is illuminated by a central skylight over the center, but the stained glass window on an angled wall provides special light and color which varies wonderfully during the day. Its simple subject matter (*Tree of Life*), growth of different forms of life, is handled very subtly in changes of color values from dark at the bottom to light at the top. I feel most fortunate to have Jack's window in my chapel. It lends great artistic quality to this small hexagonal white room

Walter Gordon, architect, September 19, 1994.

95. *Tree of Life*
    (stained glass)
    1981-82
    24 x 98

EXCERPTS FROM INTERVIEW OF THE ARTIST BY
MARYANNE CARUTHERS-AKIN
for an oral history project for Portland Center for the Visual Arts, December 1978.

You have noticed, I'm sure, the number of people who have no intention of becoming professional artists and are not doing it to learn more about art in order to go to galleries for appreciation or purchasing, but simply because they want to participate in the experience…I don't think it's any different from making music or playing music for yourself or dancing…I think a vast number of human beings really have that capability and want to be part of it…

There is a terrific kind of confusion, I believe, about who's an amateur and who isn't…A lot of these people are very unclear about their role or where it stops or starts. So that, for instance, in Portland there are a lot of amateur painters who sell a great many paintings to their friends. The friends think they know an artist, so they buy something from this person who passes himself off as an artist when he ought to be doing it just for the pleasure of doing it. And people ought to be buying from professionals but they're not…and that accounts for this huge hole in the market. These buyers do not distinguish…a lot of art is bought – enough to support all of the professional artists in this town. But much of it is amateurish and very limited in what it offers because it is done by amateurs.

I think that in the past where people at home did quilts or watercolors, there was a clear distinction about who was or wasn't a professional artist. And it was clear for the artist, too. There were guilds and professional societies. These no longer exist or no longer mean anything if they do exist. I mean, who cares about joining a professional society as an artist? They don't have clear enough standards for themselves. And it is difficult to establish such a thing stylistically. Who is really a professional? It tends to blur because professionals, themselves, often cannot tell from looking at a work whether somebody very good did it or somebody very clumsy. You have to know and see the work of the artist over a period of time. Young artists assume that someone can just look at their painting and decide it is marvelous. Well, it may be but it almost never happens like that. And nearly everyone, on a first show in New York, will get a bad review. The work cannot be evaluated in a short time, based on very little information. It all takes time, to begin to understand and see what the artist is doing or trying to do…And just as it is true of critics and reviewers, it is true of the general public. So you must go to the museums and galleries and look….

Why do people buy art? Well, they often buy a piece of the

artist. They do not look at the work and evaluate it. They have a hard time doing that. They don't have the background nor the vocabulary for that. So that, people get to know you and then they look at your work – sometimes they think about it for five or ten years before they buy something…

For a long time, I didn't sell anything. When I started selling some things, I found it rewarding that somebody wanted that or owned it, took it home, had it in his house, enjoyed it enough to keep it. Personally I dislike the idea of stacking things up in the studio – I'd rather keep prices in a reasonable range and sell my work. One reason I do prints, and small prints a lot of the time, is because it seems to me anyone ought to be able to buy something of mine. If I'm involved socially and I want that communication, then I really want to make it possible. I don't want to put my work out of my friends' range.

There is a side of people that connects them with other human beings and with other peoples' feelings and their goals and dreams. I think this is a kind of human dream that the artist is trying to be part of or to project, and he is trying to embrace other people in an experience of some kind…He is trying to move somebody…And I think that people who paint something aggressive are trying to poke other people, just like physically poking them. "Don't go to sleep…Don't die in the chair in front of the TV set." I do believe that people know there is more to life than just literal, physical things and basic necessities. Those who respond to art find it very rewarding…they find themselves a part of another world, the world of the spirit, the mind, and the emotions.

When I was in art school in 1939-40, times were very tight, very tough. And I worked part-time when I was in New York. My parents helped me and I was on a scholarship. I attended the American Artists School and I did some clean-up work and various odd jobs for the scholarship. It was a school where the teachers came in and gave their time. Most of them weren't paid. They simply came in and gave criticism. At that time, artists did not really think about making a living at art. There wasn't any possibility of doing it. But people were happy. I met Louis Bunce. He was renting a couple of rooms in his flat to students. I rented one of them. Through him I met this Portland circle that was in New York at the time: Fred and Dorothy Farr and Alton Pickens, etc. Louis had come back and had finally gotten on the WPA Mural Project. He had a very rough time getting on it, too, because you could not just come and sign up. You had to have residence for quite a long while.

Why is New York important to artists? Well, I don't think it is anymore, as far as I am concerned. But just prior to the time I was in New York, everybody went to Paris or tried very hard to go there. Paris really was the center of the art world. But at the time of World War II, the foreign artists were starting to come to New York. The situation in Europe was getting critical and so, in New York we would see Fernand Leger, Dali, etc. You might run into almost anyone. They were all coming over to escape the war. But in New York artists were still primarily painting little Picassos. So they were still about 15 years behind the times but they were closing the gap. In Louis' circle, when he was on the Mural Project, there were: Pollock, who was his good friend, deKooning, and James Brooks.

In any circle you move in, in New York as an artist or art student, you will get to know some of the people with reputations. I remember going to a little bookstore to see some work by Pollock and Rothko. The Rothko I recall was one of the beach scenes with fantastic figures in it and had very little to do with what evolved later. Abstract Expressionism had not yet started. They were on the edge of freeing themselves of that 15 year time lag and that old debt, you know…some of it was starting to happen, partly because of the War. The destruction of Paris as the art center really threw it in the laps of the New York artists. It put them in direct contact…and stirred up a kind of independence. Pollock had a lot of psychological problems and he drank like mad…but he was, I think, very open. (To fasten on his behavior) is not seeing the person at all. What he was doing was taking it in his own hands and struggling with something, while other people, lots of people, were still following the Europeans.

About the WPA: Most people were just pleased to be on the Project because, with many of them, this was the first time in maybe 30 years that they had ever just painted….they could actually spend their time painting. They had always had to work at something else…and they did everything from painting little signs for store windows and so on.

And I thought to myself that what I had to do was to simply get a job. I would be a night clerk in a hotel or something like that…something that wouldn't take all my energy or a lot of mental concentration. The thing was *I felt I would prefer a menial job of some kind rather than an interesting one or one that*

made money; because being an artist meant, you know, putting your main attention on that. And that came through very clearly to me. And I was lucky because I could do just that for a while. I could work part-time at the Dently Hotel and there was always a room and a job that would support me.

The thing that's hard for people to visualize now, I think, is that for the first 15 years out of art school, I sold only 3 paintings. And it was not at all uncommon. A few artists did better who were more sociable or who knew a little better what price to put on work, but, you know, they had to sell their work for very, very little.

In New York, if you're not on the scene and making contact with people and so on, you're not going to get the same kind of response on your work. In other words, it's an integrated kind of situation and in New York, people will say, "Well, you know you have to go to all the important shows or try to get invited there or try to get someone important to come to your show." And it is all a part of how the interest in your work might spread over a period of time.

What about my own work affects me the most? The fact that it's a very satisfying thing to do is the main thing, if somebody asks me. And when you get talking about discouraging parts of the art world, like not making a lot of money or not being tremendously successful…it's very easy to get kind of down on it. But, as a matter of fact, I never have any question in my mind about doing anything else or ever wanting to. If somebody asks me that, and they do ask because they know I am not making much money…and art students often have asked me that, I don't feel I had any alternative at all. Not so much because I was driven by insane inspiration as because it's a very satisfying use of my mind. I tend to think of it as being a way of dealing with life. I deal with what I think about and what I feel, and lots of times rather directly with what I experience and what I am seeing. And I deal with images that are nearly always recognizable – they are not realistic but they are specific in the sense that they refer to something or they derive from something observed. And they are often changed simply for their meaning or their poetry or their emotional content. No, I don't see any other job being anywhere near as fulfilling for me personally.

I suppose the hardest part about being an artist is that you have to do something else to make a living. I have spent a lot of time teaching. I've enjoyed it and I've learned a great deal, as most teachers do. Once you get started teaching, you find that you have to do some work and some thinking about yourself as well as the students. But I do regret the amount of time. I don't regret it deeply because, through the period I came up in, I was probably as fortunate as anybody could be. For a long time, our School was rather small, very intimate, with small classes and there wasn't the pressure there is in a big university. I was always involved with students who were intent on becoming artists so they were closely related in interest to my own interests. And I got into teaching by teaching a single class, a children's class, and from that I moved into a job in the Day School. At first I was extremely shy and introverted. And when Bill Givler hired me on a part-time basis, Bob Davis, the Museum Director, said, "I don't know why you are hiring that fellow. He never opens his mouth."

I arrived at the conclusion a long time ago that the title of a painting should be something that gives people a handle – not to describe it or even to tell what is there if you do not see the painting at all, but to give you a clue to it. It's very easy for people these days to simply throw up a block of some kind on painting and say, "I don't understand it." They need to see and feel as well as understand the thing and to get over the artificial hump that they cannot understand it.

I've always admired the titles of Klee's paintings, for instance, but it took me a long time to understand the painting. I found it quite alien and, though I could see it was logical, I couldn't see why it was. So, when I got used to it and to the fact that he was making visual puns – so that this singer's mouth might be like a high C, it might be like a musical note or a musical symbol – I realized that Picasso and Miro and many Europeans are perfectly willing to do all kinds of visual punning if they feel like it. They don't take it so hard! They don't have to paint a masterpiece every single time! They have enough confidence in themselves to do something that is just witty! As with Charlie Chaplin, humor is not always profound. Sometimes, something very slight can be profound and important. And that kind of released me. I have thought that with American painters (especially when sending to juried shows where they always ask for the latest and *most important work*) you see lots of paintings that are over-painted in a sense, because they are trying so hard to do something important. They cannot just relax about it.

And the kind of double imagery that grew out of surrealism was a really important discovery for me. At first, I had no idea what psychology was all about – I had to teach myself about symbolism and double imagery. And I gradually began to see that not only could it be serious, if you wanted it to be, but it could be funny as well…visual humor which had nothing to do with a by-line or a cartoon but was just a visual play, the way some objects look like others. *And I have found that kind of free play of ideas – just letting them criss-cross in any direction they want to go and produce any kind of image they want to produce without censoring them in any way, that is what I like.* I think it is crucial that you don't censor them, that you accept the ideas that arise and the things they arise in…as far as I'm concerned, something that you set out initially to dictate to is like a piece of propaganda. To me painting is much more like a poetic image. I think of something like Dylan Thomas' line, "I labor by singing light." Anybody knows what he means but singing light is not literary or literal at all. I enjoy poetry because I think it has some of that same kind of condensed imagery and it has to pack a lot into very few words. I think my kind of painting is a lot like that. It is getting a lot into a very few interrelated images some way, so that they exist together at the same time, but have all kinds of overtones and undertones they can throw off.

In talking about rejection, it is pretty hard sometimes to take criticism, as those are really your thoughts out there. It's part of you, a very basic part. I don't think you ever get over that. You learn to ignore it if it doesn't matter to you or to consider if it's somebody's opinion you respect or it seems valid for some reason. But I think you never get over somebody just saying to you, as a juror says in rejecting you…if a juror kicks me out of the Oregon Show and I have been painting for 30 years – and he says (in effect) "You're not a professional, it's no good." It's not going to throw me off very far anymore. But, unlike so many professions, I think you have to put up with that. It's not like being a doctor, where no one challenges you every time you submit to a show. *If you submit to juried shows, someone challenges you in a sense every single time unless you are right in the middle of the road.* The people who are very successful in winning prizes and being in juried shows are not the exceptional artists. They only get that after they've had recognition. The deKooning's only win those prizes after they've got a big reputation and so on.

About being rejected for exhibitions, I've sent a painting to a show and been kicked out and sent it to another show and won the purchase award for the same painting. When you go through that a few times, you can't help realizing that it's just a difference of opinion. And the opinion can vary widely. You just have to have great confidence in yourself.

ADDITIONAL REVIEWS OF THE ARTIST:

A reviewer when studying a collection of paintings by a particular artist is quite often at odds as to how to approach a proper evaluation, one that is respectful to the painter yet personal to the reviewer himself. *A reviewer is not an anonymous spectator collecting data to fill so much space in a newspaper. Copy is incidental to discovery* (emphasis added). But this discovery must take a form, express a certain quality of awareness that, while being personal, is intent on clarifying something or (some) quality in the artist's work which the reviewer thinks important. Sometimes this something, this quality cannot be explained so it must be hinted at, brought to the surface as it were, by a roundabout route.

Jack McLarty…is open to many evaluations, the most obvious is the expert use of color fitted into and working through a design framework that constantly seemed to be in a state of evolution. There is a form of incompleteness, of unfinished growth in his structures, we are surprised to find much of the work in a state of undress, at that point where the decision to be flower, plant or man has not been made; when the decision is made, the form remains rudimentary in order to emphasize a certain condition of energy or growth. The content of the work comes toward you like a flower opens, petal by petal, with light seeming to stream forth from its inception. The matte-like color surfaces, the predilection for accented edges, the sharply defined light and dark areas all shimmer in a depth that never loses contact with the two dimensional surface of the canvas….

Carl Hall, *Salem Statesman*, January 1957.

Jack McLarty, as an artist, is of all things, stubbornly unadjusted, both to his mechanized, de-personalized environment, and to the frightening flux of contemporary art. His very colorful, finely controlled and realized conceptions express by content as much as by intensity: always man, whether as child or adult, is in turmoil, this human involvement presents a thesis about the individual not usually explored in present day art movements….

(Today) esthetics is such a dogmatic master that we have tended to forget that art should, of all things, be human: that without the human visage, no matter how hidden, it is somehow barren no matter how "pure" it may be as an art form per se….Here we are witness to works that nourish the mind while delighting the eye. The intensity of thought and emotion, the supremely personal impersonal overtones in his work, whether plant or humankind, constitute the condition within which (his) sense of reality realizes itself. It is a powerful immediate sense of reality, its composition, implications are always a reflection, an intensification of his outlook on life, both in obvious understanding and that very special quality of unforeseen or unpremeditated knowledge that every painter somehow reveals in the process of growth and completion…

From a varied group of sparks of reality set in motion in a philosophical as well as a psychological space context, we are made aware of a body of ideas which almost approach myth in that they are so respectful to the truth of their continuous occurrence, their constancy in life.

Elastic principles of association, of reflection, whether they be bitter or just ironic or even futile in character, and which seem, at times, to give the appearance of a disintegrated form of imagination, flower in a free play of ideas. As in the form of poetry, the Artist seeks to achieve an organization, even a fitness to his creation: to use a quote, "I should like to peer through the center to certain basic, beautiful facts.".…It is important that we remember that the key word in this quote is '*beautiful*.'"

All of Jack McLarty's work seems to be on stage, like reality twice removed into an environment, or a room, some place where it creates its own drama, where strong lights and dark, rhythmic patterns, textural differences accent the obvious as well as the hidden portent of the activities taking place. It is a drama made up of many obscurities, and whether like that of the *Old Woman with Flowers*. which implies a state or condition of hidden activity…which yet flowers like some generative symbol, it is always submerged in a pulsating void. This submergence in environment, both as fact and as condition of mind, takes other forms…What is taking place is that all activities are submerged in their own preoccupations and activities where the line separating dream from fact is broken into unexpected implications and *we read as if they were a large tabloid all set in bold type* (emphasis added)…

Carl Hall, *Salem Statesman*, June 25, 1961.

TECHNICAL NOTES FROM THE ARTIST:

Technical information is not often included in catalogues. If the catalogue is intended as a reference, it seems worth at least an outline on technique. While craft is mostly a means to an end, it is an intimate tool for the artist and is bound into the very heart of the work.

When I first started painting in oils, the medium used was a traditional mixture of one-third linseed oil, one-third damar varnish, and one-third turpentine. This medium was used both to mix and glaze tube oil colors. All of the paintings I produced before I changed to acrylic paints were executed in this way. A simple and sound technique. Most of those paintings are in good condition today. A few have been rolled and, although correctly rolled with the painting on the outside – so that cracks will close when unrolled, some have some cracks and some flaking. This is usually due to the use of old paintings, that were painted over – some of my own and some of other students and some from the Goodwill stores. Flaking is usually from bad adhesion. Cheap canvas is often primed with a very oily base paint so it can be rolled up in art supply stores for years without developing cracks. I usually primed my own canvas and used white lead thinned with turpentine. (Do not eat these paintings!)

At the time I painted the Civic Auditorium mural, I changed to acrylic paint (1968-69). I had developed a rash on my hand and fingers that would not heal, probably from turpentine. From that time on, I have painted only with acrylics. They provided an easy way to start paintings where I used a colored tone right on the bare canvas. No priming was necessary and the ground color was matte. I prefer this to glossy surfaces, which I dislike. These paintings should never have more than a matte varnish. Some I have painted on quite a dark and absorbent ground color and these may become dull over time. If they need an acrylic matte varnish, they should be tested first by being rubbed with a damp rag or sponge across the surface, to see what the color will look like. Water will not damage the surface. Acrylic paintings are tough but they hate to be scratched. Always try to protect the surface when moving, storing or laundering them. Acrylic bonds with canvas. I have used only water as a medium.

PRINT COLLECTIONS:

Benoit College (Wisconsin)
Bowdoin College (Maine)
British Museum
Bucknell University
Calif Palace of the Legion of Honor
Davidson College (North Carolina)
Dayton Art Institute
Drury College (Missouri)
Erb Memorial Union, University of Oregon
Gilkey Collection, Portland Art Museum
Henry Gallery, University of Washington
Huntington Public Library (New York)
Indiana State University
Kalamazoo Art Institute
Kohler Art Center (Wisconsin)
Library of Congress
Linfield College (Oregon)
Mesa Community College (Arizona)
Michigan State University
Montana State University
New York Universities: Brockport, Buffalo
Museum of Fine Arts, Springfield (Mass.)
Pacific University (Oregon)
Portland Community College
Princeton University Library
Ringling Museum (Florida)
Rockford College (Illinois)
Salem Art Association (Oregon)
Salem Public Library (Oregon)
Smithsonian Institution
Southern Oregon College
Southwestern Oregon Community College
University of Georgia
University of Maine
University of Nebraska
University of New Mexico Museum
University of North Carolina
University of Oklahoma
University of Oregon Museum
University of Utah
Wittenberg University (Ohio)

MONOGRAPHS:

Griffin, Rachael. "The Metaphorical Art of Jack McLarty." *Northwest Review*, Vol. 4, No. 1, Fall-Winter 1960.

Van Cleve, Jane. "Jack McLarty: Painter as Poet." *Stepping Out Northwest*, Summer 1982: 30+.

Weber, John S. "Jack McLarty: Paintings from the Past Five Years." Oregon Art Institute, Portland Art Museum, January 1988.

PUBLIC COLLECTIONS:

Buckman School, Portland
City of Portland, Civic Auditorium
Collins View School, Portland
Erb Memorial Union, University of Oregon
First National Center Art Collection, 1st Interstate Bank
Haseltine Collection, University of Oregon Museum
Laurelhurst School, Portland
Lewis and Clark College, Portland
Lincoln High School, Portland
Mt. Hood Community College, Gresham, Oregon
Pacific University, Forest Grove, Oregon
Portland Art Museum
Portland Community College
Ridgewood School, Beaverton
Riverdale School, Portland
Salem Art Association, Salem, Oregon
Seattle Art Museum
State of Oregon, Capitol Collection
State of Oregon, Transportation Department

MISCELLANEOUS REFERENCES:

Contemporary Arts of Oregon, the Work of 40 Oregon Artists and Craftsmen. Northwest Review, University of Oregon. Eugene. Summer Issue 1959.

Griffin, Rachael. Lecture. American Association for Aesthetics, Northwest Division, Portland, Oregon, April 1961: 5-9.

Rawlins, Jane Huston. Letter to Barbara McLarty. October 1961.

Eyerly, Jack. Letter to the McLartys. 31 May 1961.

Chittick, Edna W. Letter to the McLartys. 4 March 1964.

Chittick, Edna W. Letter to Barbara McLarty. 10 July 1964.

Liepe, Madeleine R. Statement written for McLarty Exhibition, Image Gallery, March 1967.

17 Love Poems. Pat Whalen. Northwest Review. University of Oregon. Eugene. Spring Issue 1967.

McLarty, Jack. Artist's statement on creating "Emerging Woman" (woodcut) for Northwest Review. Spring Issue 1967. page 90.

Prize Winning Graphics. Book 5, 1967. Allied Publications, Ft. Lauderdale, Fla.

Ferdinand Roten Galleries Catalogue No. 9, 1967. Baltimore. page 45.

Lauha, Lillie H. Statement written for McLarty's "Auto Show," Image Gallery. 10 March 1972.

Ferdinand Roten Galleries & Aquarius Press Catalogue 1973. page 24.

Oregon Invitational Drawing Show. Fairbanks Gallery. Oregon State University. Corvallis, Oregon. March 1974.

Eiseley, Loren. Letter to the Artist. 17 April 1974.

Lakeside Editions, Catalogue 1974-75. Editor John Wilson, Lakeside Studios, Lakeside, Michigan.

Chaivoe, Nick. Statement written for McLarty Exhibition Image Gallery. August 1975.

Roy, Mayo Rae Rolph. Statement written for McLarty Exhibition, Image Gallery. August 1975.

Art for People with More Taste than Money. A competitive print exhibition. Oregon Arts Commission, Salem, Oregon 1976.

American Institute of Graphic Arts Annual Book Show 1977. New York. Limited Edition and Fine Private Press Books: Wind and Pines. Published by Image Gallery, Portland, Oregon 1977.

McLarty, Jack. Interview by Maryanne Caruthers-Akin. Oral History Project, Portland Center for the Visual Arts. 6 December 1978.

Fine Print, a Review for the Arts of the Book. Vol. V, Number II, April 1979. Calligraphic Books. Wind and Pines. Reviewer Sumner Stone.

Artquake Fifth Annual Visual Arts Exhibition. Portland. September 1981.

Healing Arts, an Exhibit of Works from the Kaiser-Permanente Collection. Portland. 1981.

Oregon Arts News, Oregon Arts Commission Salem, Oregon 1985. page 8.

New Horizons in Printmaking: East Meets West. Portland. 1986.

Artists' Liaison. 1988 Exhibition Catalogue. Venice, California. page 15.

Designed to Wear, original wearable art. Oregon School of Arts and Crafts. Portland. Poster design and program cover for 1988, 1990, 1991.

Forty Oregon Printmakers. Oregon Arts Commission/Northwest Print Council. Portland. 1988.

California Art Review. American References, Inc. Chicago. Les Krantz, Editor. 1989. pages 731, 790, 813.

Smart Art. Zephyr Press, Tucson. Patricia and Stephen F. Hollingsworth. Back cover in color.

The Art of Printmaking. Northwest Print Council. Portland. 1990.

Extinction, Left Bank #2. Blue Heron Publishing Company. Hillsboro, Oregon. Spring Issue 1992. cover illustration.

101 Prints, a benefit for Friends of the Gilkey Center and Northwest Print Council. 2 April 1993.

Art Futures. Alumni and Friends of Pacific Northwest College of Art Benefit. 8 May 1993.

CATALOGUES, EXHIBITIONS AND MUSEUMS:

Bellingham, Washington. Western Washington State College. 2nd Annual Small Sculpture and Drawing Exhibition. April 1965.

Colorado Springs. Colorado Springs Fine Arts Center. 19th Artists West of the Mississippi: The Realistic Image. August 29 to October 27, 1963.

Eugene, Oregon. Museum of Art, University of Oregon. Northwest Painters 1961, An Invitational Exhibition of Painters from Oregon, Washington and British Columbia. January 24 to February 26, 1961.

Eugene. Museum of Art, University of Oregon. Pacific Northwest Art, The Haseltine Collection. Initial Showing of the Collection. December 1-31, 1963. Eugene. Museum of Art, University of Oregon. A University Collects: Oregon Pacific Northwest Heritage. 1966. Exhibition circulated by the American Federation of Arts 1967-68.

Eugene. Erb Memorial Student Union, University of Oregon. Pacific Northwest Art Annual. Catalogues for: 1962, 1964, 1965, 1969, 1971, 1972.

Eugene. Museum of Art, University of Oregon. Statewide Services Traveling Exhibitions for 1967-68.

Eugene. Museum of Art, University of Oregon. Prospectus Supplement for Traveling Exhibitions for 1971-72.

Eugene. Museum of Art, University of Oregon. Prospectus Supplement for Traveling Exhibitions for 1973-74.

New York. Museum of Modern Art. Recent Painting USA: The Figure. 1962. Issued for the May-December Exhibition. To be shown also at the Columbus Gallery of Fine Arts; Colorado Springs Fine Arts Center; Baltimore Museum of Art; City Art Museum of St Louis; San Francisco Museum of Art; Walker Art Center.

New York. American Federation of Arts. The Drawing Society National Exhibition 1970. Participating Museums: Addison Gallery; Philadelphia Museum of Art; Cooper-Hewitt Museum (Smithsonian Institution, New York); The High Museum of Art (Atlanta); Indianapolis Museum of Art; the Museum of Fine Arts, Houston; The Art Galleries, University of California (Santa Barbara); Seattle Art Museum; Portland Art Museum.

Portland, Oregon. Portland Art Museum. Artists of Oregon. Catalogues for: 1951, 1952, 1953, 1954, 1956, 1957, 1958, 1960, 1963, 1965, 1966, 1967, 1969, 1971, 1972, 1975.

Portland. Portland Art Museum. Prints by Oregon Artists 1952. November 28, 1952 to January 4, 1953.

Portland. Portland Art Museum. Artists of Oregon: Drawings and Prints. 1956.

Portland. Portland Art Museum. 50th Anniversary Exhibition, Museum Art School (1909-1959). September 22 to October 25, 1959.

Portland. Portland Art Museum. Paintings and Sculptures of the Pacific Northwest: Oregon, Washington, British Columbia. To be shown at Portland Art Museum, Seattle Art Museum and Vancouver Art Gallery. 1959.

Portland. Centennial Exposition Building. The Oregon Scene, Oregon Centennial Painting Exhibition 1959. June 10 to September 17, 1959.

Portland. Portland Art Museum. Jack McLarty – A Retrospective Exhibition of Paintings and Drawings. September 25 to October 27, 1963. 100 works 22 illus. Foreword by Francis J. Newton. Notes by Rachael Griffin.

Portland. Portland Art Museum Faculty Exhibition, Museum Art School 1966.

Portland. Portland Art Museum. Artists of Oregon: Drawings, Watercolors and Collage. 1970.

Portland. Portland Art Museum. 10th Anniversary Show of Art Advocates (1966-1976). September 15 to October 17, 1976.

Portland. Portland Art Museum. Northwest Prints '82, the inaugural exhibition of the Northwest Print Council. October 12 to November 21, 1982.

Portland. Portland State University Gallery. Sapporo-Portland Print Exhibition, an exchange show. November 17 to December 3, 1984.

Portland. Portland Art Museum. Western States Print Invitational. July 23 to September 15, 1985.

Salem, Oregon. Bush Barn Gallery. Sixth Annual Printmakers in Oregon Invitational Exhibition. 1971.

San Diego. Fine Arts Gallery of San Diego. Pacific Coast Invitational. November 1 to November 25, 1962. To be shown also at: Santa Barbara Museum of Art, the Municipal Gallery of Los Angeles, San Francisco Museum of Art, Seattle Art Museum and Portland Art Museum.

Santa Barbara. Santa Barbara Museum of Art. Second Pacific Coast Biennial Exhibition of Paintings and Watercolors. 1957. September 10 to October 13, 1957. To be shown also at: California Palace of the Legion of Honor, Seattle Art Museum and Portland Art Museum.

Seattle. Seattle Art Museum. Annual Exhibition of Northwest Artists. Catalogues for: 1949, 1953, 1954, 1955, 1959, 1960, 1961, 1962, 1963, 1965, 1966, 1967.

Seattle. Henry Gallery, University of Washington. Northwest Print Exhibition 1958.

Seattle. Century 21 Exposition, Seattle World's Fair. Northwest Art Today: Adventures in Art. Summer 1962. Introduction by Millard B. Rogers.

Seattle. Seattle Art Museum. 35th Northwest Printmakers International Exhibition. 1964. To be shown also at Portland Art Museum.

Seattle. Henry Gallery, University of Washington. Northwest Printmakers International Exhibition 1967.

Tacoma, Washington. Madera, Tacoma, Washington. Tacoma Art League. Paintings, Sculpture and Crafts of Pacific Coast Artists, an invitational. July 1962.

Washington, D.C. National Collection of Fine Arts, Smithsonian Institution. Art of the Pacific Northwest from the 1930s to the Present. Shown February 8 to May 5, 1974. To be shown also at Seattle Art Museum and Portland Art Museum. Introduction by Joshua C. Taylor. Portland and Its Environs by Rachael Griffin. pages 3-39.

ARTICLES:

Fitzgerald, Kenneth W. "No Art in Oregon? Show to Show 'Em." Oregonian. 7 November 1948.

"New Row Over Art." Seattle Post Intelligencer. 8 October 1949 Section II.

Aaron, Louise. "New Works Arrive at Museum – Current Shows Appraised." Oregon Journal. January 1950.

Jones, Catherine. Museum, Kharouba Show Local Artists." Oregonian. 15 January 1950.

Jones, Catherine. "McLarty Work Shown." Oregonian. 18 September 1951.

"Acquisitions of Art." Portland Art Association Annual Report August 1953. pages 5 and 9.

Grondahl, Gretchen. "Artists Explore Various Media." Oregonian. 18 January 1953.

Aaron, Louise. "Jack McLarty Leads Parade with Festival Scenes." Oregon Journal. 8 March 1953.

Aaron, Louise. "Jury Discusses Oregon Art in Museum Annual." Oregon Journal. 4 April 1954.

Saarinen, Aline B. "Playground: Function and Art." New York Times. 4 July 1954.

"Brave New Playgrounds." Interiors. August 1954. page 12.

"National Citation." Oregon Artist, a journal of the Museum Art School. Vol. 2. No. 2. Winter 1954. pages 1 and 3.

Portland Art Museum Bulletin. Vol. XVII. No. 44. December 1955.

Jones, Catherine. "McLarty One-Man Show on View at Art Museum." Oregonian. February 1957.

Hall, Carl. "Oregon Artist." Salem Statesman (Salem, Oregon). June 1957.

"McLarty Art Challenging." Oregonian. 1 June 1957.

"Putting Art in Architecture." Oregonian. 24 January 1958.

Jones, Catherine. "Jack McLarty Assumes Dean's Position at Portland Museum Art School." Oregonian. 7 September 1958.

Aaron, Louise. "Art Exhibit Scheduled in Reed Lounge." Oregon Journal. October 1958.

Jones, Catherine. "Contemporary Art Discussion Planned." Oregonian. November 1958.

Aaron, Louise. "Modern Art's Impact Revealed at Forums." Oregon Journal. November 1958.

Aaron, Louise. "Many Artists Help Make Fair Attractive." Oregon Journal. June 1959.

67th Annual Report, Portland Art Association. 1959. page 17.

"Oregon Art Displayed in CPS Galleries." Tacoma News Tribune. November 1960.

Rosenthal, Jack. "For Dada's Sake Artists, Students Get Plastered." Portland Reporter. March 1961.

"How to Make a Death Mask." Portland Reporter. March 1961.

Jones, Catherine. "Artists Prepare Spoof Art Show." Oregonian March 1961.

Aaron, Louise. "Jack McLarty, Artist, Called Historian; Griffin Essay Translates Work into Words." Portland Reporter. 31 May 1961.

"McLarty Exhibition Due." Salem Statesman (Salem, Oregon). May 1961.

Hall, Carl. "Jack McLarty Exhibit at Museum Held Over." Salem Statesman. 25 June 1961.

Frankenstein, Alfred. "And Ought To Do." San Francisco Chronicle. 17 August 1961.

"Jack McLarty's Paintings Slated for Exhibit Here Next Month." The Dalles Chronicle (The Dalles, Oregon). 25 September 1961.

Aaron, Louise. "Image Gallery Opens Oregon Show." Portland Reporter. December 1961.

Rocchia, Andy. "New Portland Gallery Opens." Oregon Journal. November 1961.

"Thrills Enhance McLartys' Week." Portland Reporter. 9 November 1961.

Jones, Catherine. "How I Look to Me." Oregonian. 16 July 1961.

Aaron, Louise. "She Planned Environment." Portland Reporter. 30 December 1961.

Fagan, Beth. "Collectors Enjoy Art." Oregonian. 21 January 1962.

"Collectors Take Varied Routes on Acquiring Works of Art." Oregonian. 21 January 1962.

"Artists in 1962 Exhibition Listed." Oregonian. February 1962.

Fagan, Beth. "McLarty Exhibition, Art School Annual Due." Oregonian. 29 April 1962.

Aaron, Louise. "McLarty Utilizes Sports for Action in Paintings on Exhibition at Image." Portland Reporter. 17 April 1962.

Rocchia, Andy. "Contemporary Paintings, Lectures Enliven Art Scene." Oregon Journal. 26 April 1962.

"Work of Two Artists Picked for New York Show." Oregon Journal. August 1962.

Kietzman, Dr. Armin. "Invitational Seems Subjective, Promotional." San Diego Union. 11 November 1962.

Aaron, Louise. "Art: Viewpoint." Portland Reporter. March 1962.

"Reception at Museum Opens Exhibit of Work by Jack McLarty." Portland Reporter. September 1963.

Jones, Catherine. "McLarty Exhibition Opens at Art Museum." Oregonian. 22 September 1963.

Fried, Alexander. "The Figure Comes Back in Painting." San Francisco Examiner. 1 September 1963.

Jones, Catherine. "Jack McLarty Retrospective Show Represents 20 Years of Work." Oregonian. 22 September 1963.

Wright, Marguerite W. "Conversation Piece." Capital Press (Salem, Oregon). October 1963.

"Wall Sculpture at the Museum." Portland Art Association Calendar, Vol. 1, November 1963.

Fagan, Beth. "Comments on Artists of Oregon Exhibition at Museum Varied." Oregonian. 15 December 1963.

Fagan, Beth. "Policy Review of Oregon Show Part of Experimental History." Oregonian. 5 January 1964.

Robbins, Tom. "Jack McLarty – Too Much Sugar in the Spice." Seattle Times. 2 February 1964.

Rocchia, Andy. "Style, 'Timeless Anonymity' Artists' Goal." Oregon Journal. 17 April 1964.

"Johanson Exhibition, Newton Collection Scheduled This Week." Oregon Journal. 26 April 1964.

Rocchia, Andy. "Sound, Expressive Work in Oregon Annual." Oregon Journal. 22 April 1965.

"McLarty Exhibition Scheduled for Preview at Image." Oregonian. April 1965.

Fagan, Beth. "Artists of Oregon Prompts Views on Oregon Art Scene." Oregonian. 25 April 1965.

Grothaus, Molly. "Image Gallery Reception to Honor 3 Artists." Oregon Journal. 2 December 1965.

McLarty, Jack. "Malamud." Cover for Northwest Magazine, Oregonian. 9 October 1966.

"Portland Artist Jack McLarty Currently Showing Selected Paintings & Drawings at Art Center." Corvallis Gazette-Times (Corvallis, Oregon). January 1967.

Grothaus, Molly. "Van Hevelingen-McLarty Shows Due" Oregon Journal. 2 March 1967.

Fagan, Beth. "Mural Painting for Ridgewood School Concerns Camouflage Idea." Oregonian. May 1968.

Rocchia, Andy. "Painting Dispute Imbroglio." Oregon Journal. 2 March 1969.

Baker, Doug. "Why Not Leave to John Q. Fate of Auditorium Art?" Oregon Journal. 21 March 1969.

Rocchia, Andy. "Exhibition of Museum's Collection Sampling of Oregon Art." Oregon Journal. 15 August 1969.

"Opening Display of Auditorium Art, Forecourt Completion Coordinated." Oregonian. 1 October 1969.

"Controversial Paintings to Be Hung on Auditorium Wall." Oregonian. 23 June 1971.

"Drawings on Tour." Christian Science Monitor. New England Ed. 2 February 1971.

Kimbrell, Leonard. "Come Partake of the Feast." Oregonian. July 1972.

Fagan, Beth. "A Treasure from 8th Century Japan." Oregonian Northwest Magazine. 2 April 1978.

Avila, Penny. "Love the Same in 8th Century." Oregonian. 3 June 1979.

Gamblin, Carol. "Museum Art School: A Story of Dedication." Oregonian Northwest Magazine. 8 July 1979. pages 7-10.

Rocchia, Andy. "Artists Follow…a Trend to Refuse Trends." Oregon Journal. 17 April 1980.

Hayakawa, Alan. "Disproving Two Fine Arts Myths." Oregonian. 22 June 1980.

McGovern, Wendla. "Perceptive Art." Gallery Review (Corvallis, Oregon). September 1982.

Ullman, Sabrina. "Jack McLarty at the Image Gallery." Willamette Week. 23 November 1982.

West, Martha Ullman. "Auditorium Artworks Hidden from Public View." Oregonian. 5 August 1983.

"Public's Art Needs More Care." Editorial. Oregonian. 12 September 1983.

Campbell, Mary Ann. "Leading Artists Display Prints." Medford Mail-Tribune. 17 February 1985.

Gordon, Robert Ellis. "Going in With the Guerrillas." Clinton Street Quarterly, Vol. 7, No. 2. Summer 1985. page 49.

Hayakawa, Alan. "Oregon Galleries Challenge Accepted Ways of Marketing Art." Oregonian. 24 March 1985.

"McLarty Opens Pacific Art Season." Pacific Today, Pacific University Alumni Letter (Forest Grove, Oregon). Vol. 19, No. 1. Fall 1985.

"Printmaker Kicks Off Art Season." Hillsboro Argus (Hillsboro, Oregon). 29 August 1985.

Johnson, Barry. "Brutal Fantasies Pour Out of Jack McLarty's Acrylics at Image." Oregonian. October 1986.

"Galleries Feature Northwest Artists." The Register Guard (Eugene, Oregon). 9 July 1986.

Johnson, Barry. "McLarty's Art Shows Shocking but Original View of City." Oregonian. January 1988.

Allan, Lois. "A Confrontation with Devils." Artweek. 22 October 1988.

Johnson, Barry. "Oregon Printmakers Going Their Own Way." Oregonian. 15 July 1988.

Robinson, Andy. "Cracked." Clinton Street Quarterly, decade issue 1979-1988. page 19.

Ryberg, Barbara. "The Northwest's Blues." Artweek. 15 April 1989.

Richards, Suzanne. "Buckman Pupils Draw Conclusions About Mural." Oregonian. 7 October 1990.

"6th Annual Human Form Show at Visual Arts Center." News Times (Newport, Oregon). 9 January 1991.

Richards, Suzanne. "Unique Art Finds Homes in Portland's Schools." Oregonian. 14 February 1991.

Whittemore, L. J. "Modest Maverick." Oregonian. 24 May 1991.

Gragg, Randy. "Paul deLay Band to Add Touch of Blues to First Thursday." Oregonian. 1 May 1991.

Wyss, Judith. "McLartys Make Move." PNCA Bulletin for Alumni & Friends, 1992.

Hull, Roger. "Getting Around to Now." Salem Art Association Bulletin. August 1993.

WRITINGS BY THE ARTIST:

McLarty, Jack. "A Personal Report from New York." *Oregon Artist*, a journal of the Museum Art School, Vol. 1, No. 2, Fall 1952.

McLarty, Jack. Letter. "Bald World." *Oregonian*, 28 December 1957.

McLarty, Jack. "Art in Education." *Oregon Education Association Quarterly*, Spring 1958.

McLarty, Jack. "Charles Voorhies." *Catalogue for "A Retrospective Exhibition of Paintings and Drawings by Charles Howard Voorhies."* Portland Art Museum, 11 April 1972.

McLarty, Jack. "A Search Through Layers of Time." *Charles Heaney, Master of the Oregon Scene*, published by Image Gallery, 1980.

McLarty, Jack. "George Cummings." *Image Gallery brochure*, October 1975.

McLarty, Jack. "Eight Willamette Valley Artists Paint the Oregon Country." *Image Gallery brochure*, August 1988.

McLarty, Jack. "Circle of Influence." *Image Gallery brochure*, 6 June 1991.

LIST OF WORKS IN THE CATALOGUE:

1. *Portland* (oil) 1943 24 x 18 Collection Roger Saydack/Elaine Bernat. Shown: Retrospective Exhibition, Portland Art Museum 1963; Maude Kerns Art Center, Eugene 1986.

2. *The Orange Umbrella* (oil) 1944 41½ x 24 Collection Dennis and Shirley Schiller. Shown: McLartys' Choice 1994.

3. *Self-Portrait with the River* (oil) 1945 12 x 26 Virginia Haseltine Collection of Pacific Northwest Art, University of Oregon Museum of Art. Shown: Kharouba Gallery, Portland 1951; University of Oregon Museum of Art 1959; Retrospective Exhibition, Portland Art Museum 1963; Maude Kerns Art Center 1986.

4. *Night City with Nude* (oil) 1946 32 x 43 Shown: University of Oregon Museum of Art 1959; Retrospective Exhibition, Portland Art Museum 1963; Maude Kerns Art Center 1986.

5. *Waterfront* (oil) 1946 32 x 43 Shown: University of Oregon Museum of Art 1959; Retrospective Exhibition, Portland Art Museum 1963.

6. *City Song* (oil) 1946 36 x 18 Collection Bill and Jane Rawlins.

7. *City on Fire* (oil) 1947 32 x 43 Shown: Retrospective Exhibition, Portland Art Museum 1963.

8. *Sub-Portland* (oil) 1947 24 x 36 Collection John and Mary Louise Uchiyama. Shown: Image Gallery 1963.

9. *Conflagration Point* (oil) 1948-49 43 x 32 Shown: Retrospective Exhibition, Portland Art Museum 1963; McLartys' Choice 1994.

10. *Parade Watchers* (oil) 1949 36 x 29 Shown: Retrospective Exhibition, Portland Art Museum 1963.

11. *Barbara and Polly with a Book* (oil) 1950 43 x 32 Shown: Image Gallery 1963.

12. *Rose Parade* (oil) c. 1952 44 x 72 Shown: Retrospective Exhibition, Portland Art Museum 1963.

13. *King of the River* (oil) 1951 36 x 18 Shown: Kharouba Gallery 1951; Retrospective Exhibition, Portland Art Museum 1963.

14. *Old Woman with Flowers* (oil) 1952 40 x 20 Shown: Bush House Gallery, Salem 1961; Mt Hood Community College, Gresham 1969.

15. *The Butcher Shop* (oil) c. 1952 44½ x 36 Collection David E. Lindenberger. Shown: Image Gallery 1963.

16. *Self-Portrait as a Royal Rosarian* (oil) 1951 24 x 30 Collection Andrew Griffin. Formerly Collection Rachael Griffin. Shown: Kharouba Gallery 1951; Retrospective Exhibition, Portland Art Museum 1963.

17. *Tall Self-Portrait in Blue* (oil) c. 1953 42 x 24 Shown: McLartys' Choice 1994.

18. *Family Portrait* (oil) 1953 32 x 45 Shown: Kharouba Gallery 1953; Retrospective Exhibition, Portland Art Museum 1963.

19. *A Child's World* (oil) 1955 42 x 32 Shown: Image Gallery 1963; Mt Hood Community College 1969; McLartys' Choice 1994.

20. *The Fountain of Youth* (oil) 1959 43 x 66 Collection Lillie H. Lauha. Shown: Reed College 1960; Tacoma Art League 1962; Retrospective Exhibition, Portland Art Museum 1963.

21. *In the Air* (oil) 1959 66 x 44 Shown: Artists of Oregon 1960, Portland Art Museum; College of Puget Sound, Tacoma 1959; Ruthermore Galleries, San Francisco 1961; Retrospective Exhibition, Portland Art Museum 1963.

22. *Voyage of the Neon Horse* (oil) 1958 43 x 68 Virginia Haseltine Collection of Pacific Northwest Art, University of Oregon Museum of Art. Shown: College of Puget Sound, Tacoma 1959; University of Oregon Museum of Art 1959; The Haseltine Collection, University of Oregon Museum of Art 1963; Retrospective Exhibition, Portland Art Museum 1963.

23. *Autumn Storm (Leaf Storm)* (oil) c. 1960 40 x 48 Shown: Retrospective Exhibition, Portland Art Museum 1963.

24. *Fallen Lovers* (oil) 1960 67 x 42 Virginia Haseltine Collection of Pacific Northwest Art, University of Oregon Museum of Art. Shown: Image Gallery, Portland 1962; Retrospective Exhibition, Portland Art Museum 1963; the Haseltine Collection, University of Oregon Museum of Art 1963; University of Oregon Museum of Art 1966; Maude Kerns Art Center 1986.

25. *Rain Figure* (oil) 1961 50 x 50 Shown: Image Gallery 1962; 48th Northwest Annual Exhibition, Seattle Art Museum 1962; Retrospective Exhibition, Portland Art Museum 1963.

26. *Blue Bouquet* (oil) 1961 36 x 32 Collection Ray and Ruth Matthews. Shown: Ruthermore Galleries, San Francisco 1961; Retrospective Exhibition, Portland Art Museum 1963.

27. *Autumn Figure (Player Leaving the Game)* (oil) 1961 66 x 42 Shown: Image Gallery 1967.

28. *Run Past the Stands* (oil) 1960 48 x 37 Shown: Reed College 1960; Tacoma Art League 1962.

29. *Giant Runner* (oil) 1962-63 65 x 43 Shown: Retrospective Exhibition, Portland Art Museum 1963.

30. *The Hat Game* (oil) 1962 19 x 47 Collection Laille and Leon Gabinet. Shown: Retrospective Exhibition, Portland Art Museum 1963.

31. *World Jumper #2* (oil) 1962 66 x 42 Collection Portland Art Museum. Shown: 1962 Pacific Coast Invitational traveling to Fine Arts Gallery of San Diego, Santa Barbara Museum, the Municipal Gallery of Los Angeles, San Francisco Museum of Art, Seattle Art Museum and Portland Art Museum; Retrospective Exhibition, Portland Art Museum 1963.

32. *Little Song* (oil) 1960 45 x 34 Collection Roger Saydack/Elaine Bernat Formerly Collection Madeleine and Win Liepe Shown: 46th Northwest Annual, Seattle Art Museum 1960; Retrospective Exhibition, Portland Art Museum 1963; Maude Kerns Art Center 1986.

33. *The Anatomy Lesson* (oil) 1963 50 x 57 Shown: 1962 Pacific Coast Invitational (with *World Jumper #2*); Retrospective Exhibition, Portland Art Museum 1963; Mt Hood Community College 1969.

34. *Over the Edge* (oil) 1963 42 x 66 Collection Ingrid and Tom Rocks. Shown: Retrospective Exhibition, Portland Art Museum 1963; Corvallis Art Center 1966; Art of the Pacific Northwest from 1930 to the Present sponsored by and shown at the Smithsonian Institution, Washington, D.C. and traveling to Seattle Art Museum and Portland Art Museum 1974.

35. *Le Mabillon* (oil) 1964 42 x 66 Collection Harry and Karen Groth. Formerly Collection Mildred McGilvra. Shown: Image Gallery 1965.

36. *In the Green Region* (oil) 1964 36 x 36 Shown: Image Gallery 1965.

37. *The Lost Colour* (oil) 1965 50 x 50 Shown: Image Gallery 1965; Maude Kerns Art Center 1986.

38. *Cloak of Memory* (oil) 1965 66 x 44 Shown: Image Gallery 1965; Corvallis Art Center 1966.

39. *Tracking* (oil) 1966-67 46½ x 66½ Collection State of Oregon, Capitol Collection. Shown: Corvallis Art Center 1966; Artists of Oregon 1967, Portland Art Museum; Mt Hood Community College 1969.

40. *Icarus in Green* (oil) 1966 18 x 14 Collection Kathryn Longstreth-Brown. Formerly Collection Manuel Izquierdo. Shown: Corvallis Art Center 1966; Image Gallery 1967.

41. *Empty Runner* (oil) 1967 66 x 44.

42. *The Road Divides* (oil) 1966 68 x 44 Shown: Corvallis Art Center 1966; Faculty Exhibition, Portland Art Museum 1966.

43. *The Burden (Empty Burden)* (oil) 1967 48 x 48 Shown: Image Gallery 1967.

44. *The Junk Man* (oil) 1965 48 x 48 Collection Mayo Rae Rolph Roy. Shown: Corvallis Art Center 1966; Image Gallery 1967; Linfield College 1993.

45. *Children in the Air* (oil) 1966 36 x 30 (Detail Shown) Collection Carol and Seymour Haber. Shown: Rental Sales Gallery, Portland Art Museum 1966.

46. *Patterns of Love* (oil) c. 1968 36 x 36 Shown: Image Gallery 1968.

47. *The Red Room* (acrylic) 1969 66 x 44 Collection Laura McLarty/Keith Thompson. Shown: Artists of Oregon 1969, Portland Art Museum.

48. *Utamaro's House* (acrylic) 1969 48 x 48 Collection Charles and Hiromi McLarty. Shown: Image Gallery 1972; Hillsboro Public Library 1975.

49. *The Other Room* (acrylic) 1969 48 x 48 Collection Rodney Keyser. Formerly Collection Helen Keyser. Shown: Image Gallery 1972.

50. *The Garden of Human Possibilities* (acrylic on panel) 1969 Collection City of Portland, Civic Auditorium. This is an interior shot. The work is a double circle. It is 6′ x 6′ closed; 6′ x 12′, open.

51. *Flights of Darkness* (acrylic) 1971 44 x 66 Collection Mt Hood Community College, Gresham, Oregon.

52. *The Passing Scene* (acrylic) 1971 36 x 36 Shown: Image Gallery 1972; Hillsboro Public Library 1975.

53. *A Big Red One* (acrylic) 1970-71 66 x 44 Collection Hugh and Lisbeth McLarty. Shown: Artists of Oregon 1971, Portland Art Museum; Image Gallery 1972; Hillsboro Public Library 1975; The Governor's Invitational 1985; Maude Kerns Art Center, Eugene 1986.

54. *The Green Room* (acrylic) 1973 48 x 48 Shown: Art Advocates Show, Image Gallery 1973.

55. *Japanese Red* (acrylic) 1973 24 x 24 Collection J. Michael Deeney. Shown: Art Advocates Show, Image Gallery 1973; Hillsboro Public Library 1975.

56. *The Heart of John Donne (The Legacy)* (acrylic) 1972-73 36 x 37½ Collection Lillie H. Lauha. Shown: Art Advocates Show, Image Gallery 1973; Image Gallery 1975.

57. *Black and White Post* (acrylic on wood) 1973 71 x 10 x 10 Collection Maribeth Collins. Shown: Art Advocates Show, Image Gallery 1973; 10th Anniversary Show of Art Advocates, Portland Art Museum 1976.

58. *Light in a Room* (pastel) 1973 40 x 30 Collection Grace McDonald. Shown: Art Advocates Show, Image Gallery 1973.

59. *A Walk Through the Woods* (acrylic) 1974 29 x 41 Collection Evelyn Gordon. Shown: Image Gallery 1975.

60. *The Great Flood of 1974* (acrylic) 1974 39½ x 49.Collection Judy and Nick Chaivoe Shown: Rental Sales Gallery, Portland Art Museum 1974.

61. *General Motors (Auto-Portrait)* (acrylic) 1972 43 x 65 Shown: Artists of Oregon 1972, Portland Art Museum; Art of the Pacific Northwest from 1930 to the Present, , Smithsonian Institution, Seattle Art Museum and Portland Art Museum 1974-75.

62. *Warm Room (Dark Room)* (acrylic) c.1975 48 x 48 Shown: Image Gallery 1978; Maude Kerns Art Center 1986.

63. *The Ballad of Arn-Nicklaus* (acrylic) 1975 42 x 66 Collection Mayo Rae Rolph Roy. Shown: Artists of Oregon 1975, Portland Art Museum; The Governor's Invitational 1985; Linfield College 1993.

64. *Bus to "XoXo"* (acrylic) 1975 26 x 52 Collection Beverly and Bob Shoemaker Shown: Image Gallery 1975.

65. *Just Take the First Road* (acrylic) 1975 39 x 39 Collection Melinda Thorsnes Shown: Image Gallery 1975.

66. *Activity Along the Willamette* (acrylic) 1975 30 x 62 Collection Mary McGilvra. Formerly Collection Mildred McGilvra Shown: Image Gallery 1975.

67. *In Pretty Deep* (acrylic) 1978 36 x 36 Shown: Image Gallery 1978; Maude Kerns Art Center 1986.

68. *Chac* (acrylic on panel) c. 1983 72 x 48 Shown: Image Gallery 1986.

69. *Totems* (acrylic on wood) c. 1984 One is in the Collection of Mill Park School, a gift of the Artist.

70. *Sculpture for Artquake* (acrylic on wood) 1984 86 x 172.

71. *Underground* (acrylic) 1978 40 x 20 Collection Jack and Janet Witter. Shown: Image Gallery 1978.

72. *River City Life* (acrylic) 1979 40 x 50 Shown: Image Gallery 1986.

73. *Evidence of Passage* (acrylic) 1978 42 x 64 Shown: Image Gallery 1978; McLartys' Choice 1992.

74. *The Garden* (acrylic) 1978 40 x 60 Collection Lakeridge Junior High School, Sumner, Washington. Shown: Image Gallery 1978.

75. *Ottos on the Green* (acrylic) 1979 38 x 48 Collection State of Oregon, Transportation Department.

76. *The River Heats Up* (acrylic) c. 1980 21¼ x 41 Collection Jan and John Stahl Shown: Image Gallery 1982.

77. *The Inside/Outside Room* (acrylic) c. 1979 52 x 40 Collection Elaine Chandler. Shown: Blackfish Gallery Invitational 1986.

78. *The Prophet* (acrylic) 1982 48 x 36 Shown: Image Gallery 1982.

79. *The Dirty Babies* (acrylic) 1981 36 x 36 Collection Neil J. Moore. Shown: Image Gallery 1982.

80. *Giant in Trouble* (acrylic) 1982 48 x 37 Shown: Image Gallery 1982; Wentz Gallery, Oregon Art Institute 1988.

81. *Willamette Wars* (acrylic) 1982 40 x 50 Collection Lillie H. Lauha. Shown: Image Gallery 1982 and 1986; Wentz Gallery, Oregon Art Institute 1988.

82. *Hungry Baby* (acrylic) 1986 36 x 36 Shown: Image Gallery 1986.

83. *Red Baby* (acrylic) 1987 49 x 37 Shown: Image Gallery 1986; Wentz Gallery, Oregon Art Institute 1988.

84. *The East Side as the Garden of Eden* (acrylic) 1985 43 x 73 Collection Mr. and Mrs. James Cook. Shown: Image Gallery 1986; Maude Kerns Art Center 1986; Wentz Gallery, Oregon Art Institute 1988.

85. *Children of the Mind* (acrylic) 1987 60 x 44 Collection Mayo Rae Rolph Roy. Shown: Image Gallery 1988; Wentz Gallery, Oregon Art Institute 1988; Linfield College 1993.

86. *Blues* (acrylic) 1986 48 x 36 Collection Nelson and Olive Sandgren. Shown: Maude Kerns Art Center 1986.

87. *The Rain Queen* (acrylic) 1988 60 x 43 Shown: Image Gallery 1988.

88. *Aqua Dreams* (acrylic) 1988 45 x 40 Shown: Image Gallery 1988.

89. *Dreams of a Golf Lover* (acrylic) 1990 44 x 40 Shown: Rental Sales Galllery, Portland Art Museum 1992.

90. *World Baby* (acrylic) 1987 60 x 45 .

91. *Lynda the Cat Goddess* (acrylic) 1993 48 x 48 Collection Lynda and Michael Falkenstein. Shown: McLartys' Choice 1993; Salem Art Association, Bush Barn Gallery 1993.

92. *The New Baby* (acrylic) 1994 48 x 48.

93. *Mind Space* (acrylic on panel) 1990 7′ x 20′ Buckman School, Portland.

94. *An Unfinished Life* (acrylic) 1994 54 x 39.

95. *Tree of Life* (stained glass) 1981 24 x 98 Sacred Heart Church (chapel), Newport, Oregon.

PHOTOGRAPHY CREDITS:

Black and white photographs: Fly leaf, title page and pages 10 and 119 are by the Artist; page 5, Joseph Solman; page 6, Frank Sterrett, *The Oregonian.*

Slides of paintings in numerical order from the List of Paintings.

Brian Lincoln, Portland: Cover of "World Watcher," and numbers 14, 27, 33, 38, 48, 50, 54, 62, 63, 66, 67,68, 71, 80, 81, 82 and 93.

Roger Saydack, Eugene #1; Multi-Media, Des Moines #8; Sibila Savage, Berkeley #16; Craig Anderson, Cleveland #30; Damian Andrus, Albuquerque #40; Hugh McLarty, Vashon #53; Nick Chaivoe, Portland #61; John Stahl, Tillamook #76; Nelson Sandgren, Corvallis #86; David Strayer, Portland #94; Margaret Murray Gordon, Newport #95.

Most other slides were shot by the Artist.

ACKNOWLEDGMENTS:

This is the time and the place to give credit to those whose strong interest and support allowed us to complete this fifty year catalogue on Jack McLarty. In addition to those singled out below, we wish to thank: Lynda and Michael Falkenstein, Dennis and Shirley Schiller, and Kelton Walston.

We are greatly indebted to Andrew Griffin and Mollie Griffin Gregory who have kindly permitted us to freely use both an important monograph and the final draft of a lecture by Rachael Griffin.

Our thanks go to all who placed advance orders for the catalogue; since we have been working under close financial constraints, this was very helpful.

At the very beginning, before we were facing the hundreds and hundreds of beautiful color slides covering the paintings only, we somehow envisioned the inclusion of reproductions of some wonderful drawings and prints. Now we know that that must await another time and another catalogue. And it is likely that we will begin work on a full catalogue of the prints (in color) sometime in 1995, providing this book is as well received as we expect it to be.

Some of you will be disappointed to find your favorite painting missing here. And indeed it was distressing to us to have to make some of the final cuts. Nevertheless, we have tried very hard to include a large number of paintings that have never before been reproduced. Our intention was to gather all pertinent, available information on the Artist so that this catalogue would remain an interesting and continuing resource to all of those who possess it.

Barbara Lever McLarty
November 2, 1994

Jack and Barbara McLarty on the occasion of the 5th anniversary of the Image Gallery at 2483 NW Overton Street, Portland

About the Editor:

Barbara Lever McLarty was born in 1919 in
Alberta, Canada and has lived in Oregon since
the tender age of 2.

Co-founder and Director of the highly
esteemed Image Gallery from its opening in fall 1961
until mid-1986, she was a leading spirit behind the
energetic and unusual exhibition program of the
gallery. Because she believed the role of art dealer
should be the role of an educator, she served as an
important community resource, offering a multitude
of mostly unsung and totally unpaid services: lectures
and artists' talks, school tours, packaged shows for
small downstate art centers without resources.

During her 25 years at the Image, she issued
a consistent stream of often handsome, always
informative publications that were unprecedented:
brochures, newsletters, monographs documenting the
work of the artists she represented. Some names of
note from the roster of the Image during the sixties
and seventies are: James Castle, William Cumming,
Byron Gardner, William Givler, Robert Hanson,
Tom Hardy, Charles Heaney, Frederick Heidel,
Manuel Izquierdo, George Johanson, Hank Kowert,
Alden Mason, Richard Muller, Albert and Arthur
Runquist, Rene Rickabaugh, Charles Voorhies,
Harry Widman.

In 1966 the Image began to distinguish itself
in the field of fine, handbound books with original
prints. Much of the impetus for this came from
Clyde Van Cleve who was then designing Image
publications. His fine touch is shown in "17 Love
Poems" and in "Wind and Pines." Ms. McLarty was
to serve both as inspiration and practical muse for
five exceptional volumes that followed. Involved in
the early planning, she helped to determine content,
organized the sponsorship/financial backing, handled
all details of editing and managed the mailing and
distribution. Her editorial credits include:

"17 Love Poems"   Image Gallery (1966)

"To His Coy Mistress"   Image Gallery (1972)

"Wind and Pines"
                Art Advocates/Image Gallery (1977)

"Charles Heaney: Master of the Oregon Scene"
                Art Advocates/Image Gallery (1980)

"The Book of Color"   Art Advocates (1990)

COLOPHON

This book is set in Goudy Oldstyle Roman and Italic (Frederic
W. Goudy, 1915) by Admiral Typesetting, Portland, Oregon
and lithographed and bound by Sung In Printing, Inc.
in Korea.